ENHANCIN[ ] THINKING [ ] SOLVING FOR PRESERVICE TEACHER EDUCATION CANDIDATES AND INSERVICE PROFESSIONALS

Case Study Analysis

Erskine S. Dottin
and
Mickey Weiner

University Press of America,® Inc.
Lanham   New York   Oxford

Copyright © 2001 by
University Press of America,® Inc.
4720 Boston Way
Lanham, Maryland 20706

12 Hid's Copse Rd.
Cumnor Hill, Oxford OX2 9JJ

Library of Congress Cataloging-in-Publication Data

Dottin, Erskine S.
Enhancing effective thinking and problem solving for preservice
teacher education candidates and inservice professionals : case
study analysis / Erskine S. Dottin and Mickey Weiner.
p.   cm
Includes bibliographical references and index.
1. Problem-based learning. 2. Teachers—Training of.
I. Weiner, Mickey. II. Title.
LB1027.42 .D68   2001   370'.71'55—dc21   00-066607 CIP

ISBN 0-7618-1940-1 (pbk. : alk. ppr.)

TO

**ALL OF OUR CLASSROOM FRIENDS
IN HIGHER EDUCATION AND IN P-12
CLASSROOMS**

Contents

This case centers around an English teacher in a rural school who uses a contemporary music video to enhance her unit on Edgar Allen Poe. The intent is to illustrate Poe's point of how humans can change into monsters. Parents however feel that such videos will ruin the moral fabric of the children and seek the teacher's dismissal. The case illustrates the right of teachers to make professional decisions about what should be taught and the respect for parental and community values.

This case centers around an Hispanic child's classroom behavior. The child's teacher seeks help from the school psychologist and the child's guardians. The results are unsatisfactory. The teacher is told by the psychologist that the child's behavior is congruent with his ethnic/cultural background, and the guardian says the child simply needs more discipline. Important issues in the case include:

documenting a child's history, communicating concerns to parents, and finding appropriate resources to assist a child in the classroom.

This case centers around an adolescent boy whose teacher perceives him as working below his ability. She takes up the cause of this young man as her own personal mission. The child, however, may not need help. The teacher may be looking for a problem that is not really there. She feels sorry for the boy, and, like Don Quixote, wants to fight for what she perceives as right.

This case centers around a teacher's classroom procedures that allow for a more differentiated curriculum and individualized expectations in a dropout prevention class. Two students' tests contain fewer questions than the tests for the rest of the students who perceive this difference as unfair. Important issues in the case include: how teachers deal with individual differences and how they address the affective domain in the classroom. This case also focuses on what is "fair" when accommodating students' individualities.

This case centers around a young girl's adjustment to kindergarten. An overprotective mother hinders her child's academic and social progress by interfering with the child's schoolwork and attendance. The mother constantly questions the teacher's judgment and abilities. This inhibits the child from developing independence and becoming a responsible learner. The main issue in the case revolves around a parent's lack of trust in a teacher's professional expertise. It also deals with conflicting perspectives between the school and the home regarding the child's educational needs.

This case centers around a Catholic school teacher's conflict between the school's policy and her conscience as a professional who cares about the needs for her students. The school does not allow teaching about responsible sexual behavior. There is, however, a need to give students information to make responsible choices, since there is a high rate of teenage pregnancies in the community. The central issue in this case concerns a teacher's ability to navigate between accommodating the needs and requirements of the school, the students and the teacher.

This case centers around a philosophical difference of opinion in the correct placement of a student with low academic ability and behavioral problems. An experienced teacher, who runs a well-organized classroom, feels the student belongs in a special school; a younger teacher, whose environment is less structured, feels the student does well in a regular school setting. The bottom line of the problem is what is the best school environment for the student. State and federal law state that a student be placed in the least restrictive environment for his/her special learning needs.

This case centers around a school guidance committee that is not functioning properly. One of the members, a teacher, feels she can help, but her solution runs counter to the laissez-faire attitude of the principal, and the frustrations of the other committee members. The roles of the faculty, teachers and counselors on the committee are seen as separate and ill-defined. The main issues of this case revolve around: *communication* (role and responsibilities not being clearly defined), *school climate* (the school seems to be without a common purpose or mission), and *ethics* (falsification of documents so students can receive attention and services).

This case centers around a teacher searching for a solution to improve the academic performance of a student who lacks self-confidence and is alienated from his peers. Low teacher expectations in the past, and the student's socioeconomic status attribute to the student's behavior. The teacher's approach in managing the learning environment is unsuccessful despite her attempts to use various instructional techniques. The issues in this case also deal with updating teacher training, developing communication with parents, discovering a student's interests and talents to better motivate the student, as well as, getting other teachers' and students' input.

This case centers around a fifth grade teacher's concern that she cannot fully meet the needs of a handicapped student in her class. The teacher has a conference with the principal and the student's parents to discuss her concerns. The case also deals with funding and pressures involved in a pilot program. Attitudes and adjustment to a new program by teachers and students play a role here also. Another issue in the case is effective parent communication and support of the school's administration in resolving the situation. Other important issues include: mainstreaming, cooperative group work and building a community of learners.

Preface

This book is written with the hope that pre-service teachers and in-service professional educators will participate in learning communities as means toward enhancing their professional growth. Society in the world of western philosophy pursues the "virtues" of competition; in the world of eastern philosophy the road to personal enrichment is through the "virtues" of cooperation in harmony with others and one's environment.

As teachers and learners invest themselves in collaborative group approaches, they develop a firmer sense of their own identity. Teaching and learning problems identified and delineated through cooperative interaction appear to challenge people to produce creative solutions, and to become more creative individuals.

As pre-service and in-service professionals work together to search for solutions to problems in the field of education, the hope of the authors of this book is that they will build professional relationships with each other based on mutuality, and will therefore contribute to the further professional development of each other.

A learning community is not a locality where people reside. Rather, a learning community implies commonality, gregariousness, and shared enjoyment that facilitate the exchange of experiences.

Acknowledgments

We are truly indebted first and foremost to the teacher education candidates at the University of West Florida who willingly volunteered to share their ideas regarding the elements of cases. It was that sharing and discussion that brought to fruition the cases in this book.

We are also indebted to the teacher education candidates at Florida International University who in completing their performance tasks in EDF 3515 Philosophical and Historical Foundations of Education concurrently provided the lessons from which insights to improve the cases and analysis process emerged.

More specifically, we are indebted to the wonderful teachers at South Pointe Elementary School on Miami Beach who went out of their way to offer insights and analyses of each of the cases.

Introduction

If learning is the acquisition of personal meaning then learning to think and communicate is a vital aspect of a meaningful education. On the other hand, if education is largely about asking important questions and finding fundamental answers to those questions then we may learn to recognize the truly important questions in order to make sense of the world around us by (a) understanding information (b) solving problems (c) working towards goals and (d) making sense of our surroundings to improve them. Thinking is the way we make sense of the world. Thinking critically and creatively is thinking about our thinking so that we can expand, clarify and improve it.

Helping teacher education candidates to make sense of the world of teaching and thereby increase the possibility of their improving that world should command a certain priority in teacher preparation programs. However, many teacher education candidates have not been provided the thinking strategies to do so, even though it would seem that the central role of the formal educational system should be to teach those strategies. [1]

One of the necessary components of a good teacher education curriculum is critical analysis. According to Kennedy (1988), this means to engender in teacher education candidates the ability to critically analyze situations, and generate multiple interpretations, and the ability to formulate deliberate action plans that result from critical analysis. Professor John Goodlad reinforces the foregoing when he suggests that "Programs for the education of educators must engage future teachers in the problems and dilemmas arising out of the inevitable conflicts and incongruities between what works or is accepted in practice and the research and theory supporting other options" (Goodlad, 1990, 192).

This book focuses on the use of the case method to engender higher order thinking regarding the knowledge base on which best practices in teaching and learning rest. Its aim is to enhance critical analysis knowledge, skills and dispositions of teacher education candidates and "engender in ... beginning teachers a sense of possibilities as well as a sense of what is; an awareness of multiple realities present in classrooms, not as 'given' but as 'made' (Florio-Ruane and Clark, 1990).

Problem Solving and Critical Thinking

Two of the strategies to facilitate a meaningful education are problem solving and analyzing. A problem is basically a question or situation that presents uncertainty, perplexity or difficulty. It is a matter that requires solution, for until a solution is reached, the problem remains a problem. No problem can be satisfactorily resolved by dealing only with its symptoms. A symptom is something caused by a problem, it is not the cause of the problem.

Analyzing involves an analysis of issues. The focus of analysis is to seek answers to such questions as "what is the issue?" "what is the evidence related to the issue?" "what are the arguments concerning the evidence?" and "what is the conclusion about the issue?"

The use of cases with teacher education candidates may thus facilitate their engaging in performance tasks, which require the use of critical, and creative thinking strategies to raise and answer important questions in education.

Problem Solving Model

John Dewey in his book How We Think suggests that thinking be stimulated by the occurrence of a problem. He contends that knowledge about the world is acquired when one begins an observation and inspection of problem and the facts related to the problem so that one may locate and clear up the problem: in other words, to gain some tentative truth about the problem. However, for one to gain that tentative truth about the problem, Dewey goes on to indicate that one must formulate an hypothesis or suggestion of possible solution to the problem together with the elaboration of that hypothesis by reasoning. Then one must test the related ideas derived from the foregoing process and use the results of that testing as a guide to new observations and experimentation (Dewey, 1910).

In a more contemporary context, Loren Thompson in his book Habits of the Mind: Critical Thinking in the Classroom lays out a sequential problem solving model that embraces both problem solving and analyzing as strategies for facilitating meaningful education. Thompson argues that a process in which one first begins by determining whether the problem can be defined may formulate good habits of mind. His suggested sequence for problem solving next focuses attention on (a) the question of what is known about the problem (b) what is not known that may be important (c) what assumptions can be made regarding the problem and (d) dividing the problem into logical parts and using critical thinking skills to solve each part (Thompson, 1995).

The underlying problem solving model in this book is an adaptation of both Dewey's and Thompson's models of thinking and problem solving. Meaningful education is facilitated for teacher education candidates as they examine cases that are controversial in nature and challenge beginning teacher educators to think analytically and thoughtfully about the experiences the cases describe. The problem solving sequence being advocated will push teacher education candidates to learn to do the following through case analysis:

1. Place educational problems in the case(s) in particular definitional categories (for example, local as opposed to state control; parental participation in schools and educators' responsibilities; instructional strategies or curriculum delivery).
2. Identify known factors about the problem as articulated in the case(s).
3. Explain and offer justification for factors related to the problem that are not directly known from the case but are just as important to understanding the problem in the case. This process requires candidates to define educational problems by their social, philosophical, political, economic, legal, psychological, etc. factors. In other words, candidates will learn to draw upon theoretical and/or empirical work and craft knowledge to help them support claims of the factors' related importance.
4. Explain things taken for granted in the case.
5. Identify underlying arguments in the case and be able to check the reasoning in each argument vis-à-vis validity and errors in reasoning.
6. Offer their own interpretations for educational problems by highlighting the underlying problem(s) in the case, offering interpretations of the significant issues in the case (theoretical, empirical, etc.), noting the weaknesses in the problem they want to avoid and assumptions they do not accept, and then offering their own solutions to the problem by drawing on professional knowledge of best practice to support their solution(s).

Problem Solving and Enhancing Teacher Knowledge

Cochran-Smith and Lytle (1999) maintain that:

... the knowledge teachers need to teach well is generated when teachers treat their own classrooms and schools as sites for intentional investigations at the same time that they treat the knowledge and theory produced by others as generative material for interrogation and interpretation. In this sense, teachers learn when they generate local knowledge *of* practice by working within the contexts of inquiry communities to theorize and construct their work and to connect it to larger social, cultural, and political issues (250).

This form of teacher knowledge seems consistent with that gained through problem solving, and problem-based learning. In this context, questions about teaching and learning are always subject to discussion, and knowledge gained from such discussion and analysis is according to Cochran-Smith and Lytle (1999) "... constructed in the context of use, intimately connected to the knower, and although relevant to immediate situations, also inevitably a process of theorizing" (272-273).

The Need for the Book

The call for the use of the case method in the preparation of teachers has been quite evident in the early calls for teacher education reform in America (Carnegie Commission, 1986; Education Week, March 28, 1990; Shulman, 1989). These calls have prompted the development of several case strategies (Broudy, 1990; Greenwood, 1989; Jackson & Ormrod, 1998; Kowalski, Weaver & Henson, 1990; McAninch, 1993; Silverman, Welty & Lyon, 1992; Shulman & Colbert, 1988). On the other hand, the need to enhance the thinking skills of teacher education candidates and in-service professionals has been addressed directly by, among others, Clabaugh, 1997; Eggen & Kauchak, 1988 and Thompson, 1995. What is needed is a book that utilizes the case method of learning to enhance teacher education candidates' and in-service professionals' problem solving abilities and their ways of thinking critically through analysis of arguments and errors in reasoning, and the sharing of analyses.

Case Analysis in Action: The Process

You are a teacher in a suburban high school. You feel that the performance of the students in your class is poor and you give the majority of the class C, D, and F grades in spite of the fact that the class is considered college preparatory. The father of one of your students, to whom you gave a D grade for the semester, comes to discuss his child's progress and the grades given in your class. He is very concerned about the low semester grade and does not believe his child deserved to get such a low grade. He suggests to you that you should be more flexible in your evaluation of students and you should change his child's grade to at least a C, so that his child's chances of getting into a good college will not be ruined. He makes a point of stressing the fact that his child is a hard worker but not a quick learner, a point that you openly agree is true. At the end of the conference, the father mentions that he is an established, influential member of the community and has friends on the School Board. What will your reaction be?
Taken from: Brubaker, D.L.& Simon, L.H. (1993). Teacher As Decision-Maker: Real-Life Cases to Hone Your People Skills. California: Corwin Press (144).

According to John Dewey (1910) thinking starts with reflection when a person perceives some sort of problem. He predicted that the person's feeling of puzzlement normally precipitates, on the part of the person, observation, collection of data, and suggestions for a solution to the problem.

The following process is a means by which critical reflection on educational matters may be conducted. To facilitate the process, as a cooperative reflective endeavor, participants engaged in the case analysis first respond, on their own, to steps one through five. These responses then become the catalysts for step by step group dialogue. At the conclusion of the dialogue on steps one to five, participants, either as a group or as individuals, complete step six, by providing a comprehensive interpretation of the case. The material and knowledge for this interpretation should come from the reflective dialogue on steps one to five.

Step 1: Defining the Problem

The first step in the case analysis process is to <u>tentatively</u> define the problem. Caution must be taken, however, to avoid the identification of the symptom(s) of the problem and not the problem itself. No problem can be satisfactorily resolved by dealing only with its symptoms. A symptom is something caused by a problem, it is not the cause of the problem.

For example, many students when presented with the foregoing case suggest that the definitive problem is about how grades should be given. However, the giving of grades is symptomatic of a larger problem vis-à-vis how learning should be assessed. In the case, the problem seems more to be about parental involvement in schools, and more specifically, about the right of teachers to be able to make professional judgments about student learning without their judgments being second-guessed by parents.

The gathering of data and further analysis, in the process, will provide the opportunity to acquire a much clearer understanding of the true nature of the problem. This step, therefore, is intended to help one highlight the major element(s) of the case.

Step 2: Identifying the Facts in the Case

This step may be considered the inspection of facts phase. Thompson (1995) in his problem solving model refers to this phase as the "what do we know about the problem?" aspect of the case. In the foregoing case, individuals might have come to the group dialogue with some of the following and/or group dialogue might lead to the recognition of the following facts in the case:

- The teacher is in a suburban high school.
- The teacher gives the majority of the class C, D and F grades.
- A particular student received a D grade.
- A parent wants to discuss his child's progress and grades received since he is concerned about his child's low semester grade.
- The teacher and parent agree that the student is a hard worker but not a quick learner.
- The class is considered college preparatory.

Step 3: Understanding the Problem

Being able to make connections to things not directly stated in the case, but which have a direct bearing on the case, is a vital phase in case analysis. This phase enables one to draw upon one's knowledge base in education. Research has shown that the more sophisticated a teacher's knowledge base, the more enhanced is his/her decision making ability. In other words, how students conceptualize and frame problems of professional practice reveals a great deal about their professional knowledge and developing theoretical practice (Doebler, Roberson & Ponder, 1998).

This phase of the case analysis should bring to the fore candidates' professional knowledge (content, philosophical, historical, psychological, pedagogical, sociological, legal, etc.) or lack thereof about the underlying connections in the case. In fact, the use of the case method should help in stimulating the candidates' growth in professional knowledge - theoretical, social, self, experiential, subject matter, content-specific pedagogy, class organization and management, and student-specific pedagogy (Connelly & Elbaz, 1980; Geiger & Shugarman, 1988).

Case participants use this step to first on their own identify things in the case that are not directly stated but are quite germane to understanding the case. During the group dialogue, participants first concur about underlying issues in the case that are critically related but not directly stated in the case. Participants then determine their knowledge levels regarding each related issue. What theoretical, empirical, or craft knowledge can they provide to support the relevance of the issue to the problem? They determine how they might go about acquiring such knowledge about those related issues of which they can provide little support?

In this case the following issues are not stated directly in the case but may be deduced from the case and are relevant to understanding the case:

- what kinds of assessments were used to determine student performance?
- what criteria were used by the teacher to determine grades: Is there a school or district policy on how grades are determined?
- what subject is being taught: Is it an honors class; an advanced placement class?
- what is the ethnic and social make up of the class?

- is the student male or female?
- has the teacher had previous conferences with parents: Does the teacher normally have parent-teacher conferences: What is the school or district's policy regarding parent-teacher conferences: Did the student attend the conference the teacher had with the parent: What materials were shared at the parent-teacher conference?
- is the parent's evaluation of what students deserve for their performance based on criteria shared with the parent or simply on the parent's opinion and/or bias?
- what is the student's grade level?
- is the parent's call for flexibility in evaluation predicated upon the teacher's use of normal probability measures?
- does the parent want all other hardworking students to have their grades changed?
- what is the basis for the teacher's and parent's conclusion that the student is a hard worker but not a quick learner?
- is there any precedent of School Board members influencing teachers to change grades or of their using their authority/power to demand changes?
- what is the district's policy regarding teachers' contract?
- is the teacher a member of the teacher's union?

Once the case analysis group has agreed to the relevance of the foregoing issues the next step requires the assessment of the group's knowledge base regarding the issues. What theoretical, pedagogical, or professional knowledge can or does the group use to make connections between the problem and the foregoing things that may be important to understanding the problem?

The work of Doebler, Roberson and Ponder (1998) indicates that the further along candidates are in their teacher education programs the more sophisticated should be their ability to draw on theoretical, pedagogical and/or professional knowledge and understanding to assist them in making problem solving decisions.

This phase of the problem solving process highlights a vital aspect of what some refer to as "problem-based learning" (Savery, 1994). One of the aspects of problem-based learning is to enhance learners' development of content knowledge through the use of real world situations or problems (Aspy, Aspy & Quimby, 1993).

This phase of the problem solving process thus enables learners to develop and engage in search strategies to enhance their knowledge of the related and underlying issues in the case. As they work with each other in the search for information, the instructor has the opportunity to help learners see the benefits of sharing ideas and information. Such sharing enhances the need for social interaction and the development of inter- and intra-personal skills.

Finding information in this information age may be facilitated by one's level of information literacy. According to Carr (1998) critical thinking, problem solving and decision making enhance the kind of cognitive skills "necessary to create new knowledge and to learn how to learn ... a key characteristic of those who are information literate" (1). This phase of the problem solving process may thus contribute to information literacy development for teacher education candidates.

Giving the foregoing relevant issues to the case that were identified, case participants could share their knowledge, and seek knowledge when and where appropriate (theoretical, empirical, professional) of the following case related ideas:

- authentic assessments, standardized tests
- the distinction between grades and evaluation
- college preparatory curriculum and electives; tracking and ability grouping
- the impact of socioeconomic factors on learning
- gender bias in schools
- parent-teacher collaboration
- the use of assessment rubrics
- cognitive development and learning
- norm-references versus criterion-referenced measures
- equity in the classroom
- objective test results; subjective performance indicators; classroom observation
- power and influence in schools
- professional rights of teachers regarding contracts
- teachers rights regarding union participation

Step 4: Finding Assumptions

Finding things taken for granted is a critical skill in problem solving. Many human actions are predicated upon unstated ideas, that is, things taken for granted. However, since assumptions may be valid or invalid, acceptable or unacceptable, then it is important to identify unstated things taken for granted so that they may be examined. For example, if an assumption behind an argument is invalid or unacceptable then the whole argument may be worthless.

In educational matters certain value systems may be assumed in the discussion of problems or in responses to events, things, etc. Examining carefully the things taken for granted by key actors or situations in cases is therefore a salient component of the problem solving process.

Imbedded in the foregoing case are several unstated ideas among which are:

- students in the class have received other low grades for the semester.
- students in college prep classes do not normally receive low grades.
- good performance earns students a grade of B or better.
- student performance is correlated with academic performance (cognitive) and not with affective or psychomotor performance.
- to get into a good college high school students must have a grade of C or better.
- grades are the main admissions criteria used by colleges.
- grades are good predictors of success in college.
- student progress is related to academic progress and not to social, emotional, and/or ethical progress.
- the parent's call to change the grade is applicable only to his child.
- the student wants to attend college.
- the teacher has an inflexible system for evaluating student performance.
- the parent can use his influence to affect the classroom discussions of the teacher.
- school board members will side with parents and not with teachers.

- perceived classroom problems in a school can be resolved without involving the school's administration.
- the parent-teacher conference did not provide the parent with the kind of action he wanted.
- school board members, without affording teachers due process, can influence their classroom decisions.

Examining these assumptions will further enhance teacher education candidates' critical thinking abilities, and as a result afford them the opportunity of developing sounder options to resolve the problem. Are the assumptions valid? Is there evidence that might confirm the validity or invalidity of these assumptions?

Some of the assumptions are specific to the events in the case. As a result, the evidence to prove their validity or invalidity must come from the case information. On the other hand, there are some things taken for granted in the case which have a more general application: for example, the assumption that students in college prep classes do not receive low grades may be challenged by data and information from outside the case.

Step 5: Detecting Arguments

> Our job as thinkers ... is to recognize and assess the relative merits or shortcomings of a point of view in the interest of greater understanding of ideas, ourselves and others. Understanding that the large questions and issues we face are comprised of a myriad of points of view is the first step to rationally and fair-mindedly assessing and then evaluating various points of view---and, it is essential for engaging in fruitful dialogue in the interest of maturation, problem solving and good judgment. (Danny Weil of the Critical Thinking Institute, Guadalupe, California)

A good thinker, when he or she hears or reads certain types of materials, will immediately ask questions such as: What is the point of view being expressed? What are the arguments being advanced? Are these arguments supported? Do assumptions, hidden or otherwise, lurk behind statements? Do any obvious fallacies appear? Are terms defined and used consistently or does meaning shift consciously or unconsciously?

Effective thinking and problem solving involves identifying underlying arguments and checking the validity of those arguments (the structure of the arguments) and the content of the arguments (informal fallacies).

There are four salient arguments in the foregoing case. Three of the arguments may stated as deductive, hypothetical arguments, and the fourth may be stated as a deductive, categorical argument:

Argument 1: If a teacher determines that student performance is poor then he/she should give low grades; the performance of the majority of students in a college prep class is poor; therefore, the students should be given low grades.

Argument 2: If one does not get good grades then one's chances of getting into college are diminished; my child's grades are low; therefore, my child's chances of getting into college are diminished.

Argument 3: If one works hard then one should be rewarded; my child is a hard worker; therefore, my child's grade of D should be changed to a C.

Argument 4: Teachers' professional judgment can be overridden by School Board members who cater to the wants of their friends in the community; I have friends on the School Board and I am an influential member of the community; therefore, I can use my influence to get the teacher to change my child's grade.

Are the arguments useful in helping to find solutions to the case? If they are valid structurally (which arguments one, two and three are), but contain errors in reasoning (informal fallacies in all four - *non sequitur*), then such weaknesses in reasoning in offering solutions to the problem should be avoided. See Appendix for learning more about the process of analyzing arguments.

Final Step: Offering Interpretations and Solutions

Problem solving presupposes the examination of options, that is, solutions to resolve the problem. A prerequisite in offering solutions is that (1) any proposed solution should relate directly to the nature of the problem, and (2) the proposed solution can be defended with evidence from reliable sources. In the case of schooling and classroom problems the solution should be justified through theoretical, empirical, and/or craft wisdom knowledge.

The process, steps 1 to 5, which may be construed as the notes collection stage, affords problem solvers the opportunity to obtain a much clearer understanding about the real nature of the problem.

In this case, if they conclude that their initial identification of problem elements are still correct (for example, the assessment of learning; parental involvement in schools; and the right of teachers to make professional judgments about student learning) then they can identify the salient issues that need to be resolved and the constraints which place parameters on their actions. The solutions chosen will then minimize the undesirable conditions in the problem.

This step enables the group or individuals to provide a comprehensive interpretive narrative of the case. For example, an interpretation of the foregoing case might be:

Interpretation of Case

The case centers around (a) a teacher in a suburban high school who gives the majority of students in her college preparatory class C, D and F grades, and (b) a parent of one the students who receives a D who is dissatisfied with his child's grade and seeks to influence the teacher to change it.

The case clearly highlights the use of grades as the single measure of student learning, and the right of teachers to make professional judgments about student learning without being second-guessed by parents.

The parent's behavior reinforces the point made by Levine and Levine (1996) that "Realizing that an avenue of opportunity is provided by the educational system, parents have encouraged their children to continue further and further in school" (35). More so, it seems that part of the underlying motive of the parent is to see education, in this case going on to college, as a channel to social mobility and a better economic status for his/her child. It is no surprise to find the parent, therefore, offering veiled threats to the teacher to change his/her child's grade. The parent seems oblivious to the data which indicate that "only about one-third of seniors in the highest quartile on test performance graduate from college four years later" (Levine & Levine, 1996, 36). The parent's underlying argument appears to be that since his child got a low grade in a college preparatory class, therefore the child's chances of getting into college are diminished. Of course the argument begs the question since one low grade does not a college career diminish or deter. Current college admissions realities would indicate that:

(1) grades are not the single admissions criterion used by colleges
(2) grades in and of themselves are not necessarily good predictors of one's success in college.

On the other hand, the case offers the teacher a wonderful opportunity to review her ideas regarding the assessment of student learning. While school districts generally establish standards for reporting student academic progress through academic grades, the recent push for authentic assessment of student learning has provided teachers the opportunity to let students demonstrate their learning through authentic tasks instead of simply through standardized or objective tests.

Solution(s)

In this case, the following are viable solutions:

- The teacher might justify her assessment measures by connecting her philosophy of teaching, student learning outcomes, and her knowledge about how students learn. The paradigm shift in education from a teaching model to a learning model, that is, the need to know what students have learned, necessitates, on the part of the teacher, clarity of pedagogical purpose, knowledge of desired learning results and appropriate assessment measures.
- The teacher might share with the parent evidence of her scholarship of the classroom, that is, her knowledge and skills of strategies to improve poor student performance and her involvement in a professional learning community with her peers.
- The teacher might discuss with the parent legal precedent regarding grading and connect her assessments to the school's mission and standards and school's policies and procedures vis-à-vis grading.
- The teacher might review with the parent her level (degree and kind) of communication with the parents of her students in general, and reinforce how her strategies vis-à-vis her professional collaboration with parents are fostering the kind of the climate conducive to her having an impact on student learning.

Case Analysis Learning Strategies

Case analysis of real schooling situations and practices is a strategy for enhancing effective thinking and problem solving skills. Case analysis in this book is also intended to help learners acquire relevant content knowledge of the social, historical, philosophical, curricular, legal, political, psychological, and economic dimensions of education.

Learners in this process must take more responsibility for their learning than in traditional learning situations. The teacher must be more of a facilitator and co-learner, assisting learners, when necessary, with guidance, and germane resources.

The analysis of the cases is best done as a group project. This enables learners to first have general discussions of the case(s) by utilizing the problem solving and critical thinking case process. To use the case analysis process, the group members may first on their own determine the nature of the problem, ascertain the facts in the case, and identify issues, themes and/or ideas and concepts that are not known in the case but may be very relevant, underlying assumptions and arguments.

The large group may then engage in dialogue about the members findings for steps one to five in the case analysis process. The teacher may act as a co-learner here in helping the group with the strategy of concept mapping to create a web of related issues, themes, ideas and concepts in the case, and with direction for gathering related content knowledge vis-à-vis the identified issues, themes, ideas and concepts.

Finding assumptions and analyzing the arguments in the case may be assigned to different group members and then discussed as a large group with the instructor. Finally, the entire group may engage in the discussion of appropriate solutions. The soundness of the group's offerings must be based, however, on the relationship of the solution to the problem and the group being able to defend its proposed solutions with theoretical, empirical and/or craft wisdom evidence. Doebler's work on the impact of case study on the level of student decision making suggests that teacher education candidates become more sophisticated in their use of knowledge, theories, principles, etc. in solving cases as they progress through teacher preparation programs that use a problem-based learning approach (Doebler, 1998).

Instructors might therefore assess candidates' learning in case analysis by doing a comparative content analysis of the pre case analysis and the interpretation and analysis provided at the end.

They might examine the following:

(a) the aspects of the problem that were attended to.
(b) the options/solutions generated in resolving the problem
(c) the types of knowledge drawn upon to develop and evaluate the options/solutions
(d) the use or lack thereof of theoretical principles, principles of practice, etc. In other words, the use of context/situational knowledge, theoretical knowledge, social knowledge, self knowledge, and experiential knowledge (Connelly & Elbaz, 1980).

Another evaluative option is to utilize a rubric that outlines expected standards of performance. Some suggested criteria for assessment of learning are:

Exceeds Standard:
Group Work - goes after material with little motivation; actively works to broaden knowledge base of the problem.
Quality of Work - shows convincing evidence of understanding the nature of the problem; analyses and explanations are justified; solutions show convincing evidence of knowledge of the realities of education and schools.
Meets Standard:
Group Work - needs some direction to seek out materials; demonstrates some attempt to broaden knowledge base of the problem.
Quality of Work - shows clear evidence of understanding the nature
of the problem; some analyses and explanations are justified; solutions show evidence of knowledge of the realities of education and schools.
Below Standard:
Group Work - shows little evidence and motivation to seek out materials; does not work to broaden knowledge base of the problem.
Quality of Work - shows little understanding of the nature of the problem; analyses and explanations are not justified; solutions do not show evidence of knowledge of the realities of education and schools.

Notes

1. Some of the strategies to facilitate meaningful education include: (1) problem solving, (2) decision making, (3) conceptualizing, (4) analyzing, (5) ethical testing, and (6) understanding information.

Case 1

It is spring at Pointe High School. Pointe is a rural area with a divergent population of Seminole Indians, Mexican migrants, a largely impoverished African-American population, and a small Caucasian population that is comprised of poor and elite farm families. The common cultural element of this community is its ultraconservative population. Although racial discrimination is present, and drugs dominate the scene, the parents disregard the pressures that are changing the youth, and work to maintain a conservative stance, and do what is "right" for the community.

The high school is a large impressive structure, even more impressive with the addition of the new auditorium, next to the main building. The principal, a gentleman in his mid-forties, prides himself for running a "tight" ship but being fair to teachers and students alike. Today, however, a distraught parent, who is also a newly elected member of the school board, sits in the principal's office. She indicates that several parents in the district have spoken with her demanding that the principal dismiss the new English teacher,

Parent: "I am sorry to disturb you, sir, but it has been brought to my attention that the new English teacher, Ms. Jones, has shown the music video 'Thriller' in her classroom."

Principal: "I was not aware of this; however, I am not sure I see the problem. Have you spoken with Ms. Jones?"

Parent: "Well, as a parent, and a member of the school board, I feel that such satanic, demonic, and unorthodox practices must be stopped before the moral fabric of the children is ruined."

Principal: "I understand your concern for the children. But what exactly are you suggesting?"

Parent: "I want Ms. Jones fired immediately."

Principal: "I understand your reasoning, mam. On the other hand, I hope you understand my position as the principal of our school; I will have to check into the matter before any final decisions are made."

After the parent leaves, the principal calls in the English Department Chairperson to discuss the situation. The English Department Chair, a teacher with eighteen years experience, is not only loved by the students, but also respected by the faculty. She is also considered to be a "liberal" but has never done anything disruptive in the classroom. She keeps her views to herself.

The English Department Chair is also completely unaware of Ms. Jones' use of the "Thriller" video but tells the principal that she will talk with Ms. Jones immediately, and find out what is actually going on.

In an after-school conference, The English Department Chair talks with Ms. Jones and finds, as she suspected, that Ms. Jones acted innocently.

Chairperson: "Ms. Jones, I apologize for keeping you after today's classes. We have a small problem. A parent is quite upset about your showing a particular video in your classroom."

Ms. Jones: "I have shown numerous videos to my students."

Chairperson: "Yes, but most of the videos are a part of the approved curriculum--in one way or another--are they not?"

Ms. Jones: "Yes."

Chairperson: "Well, unfortunately, the video I am referring to is not."

Ms. Jones: "Then you must be talking about the music video 'Thriller'. It was the number one video a few years ago."

Chairperson: "Precisely. On the other hand, this parent seems to think that this video will 'ruin the moral fabric of the children.' What do you think?"

Ms. Jones: "I do not agree. I was simply trying to update the Edgar Allen Poe unit with a contemporary video which illustrates how humans can change into 'monsters.' I thought the video would enable my students to relate better to the macabre imagery of Poe. Besides, ghost stories and movies have probably been heard and seen not only by the students but also by their parents; and high school students can certainly separate fact from reality."

Ms. Jones also makes it clear that she should be allowed academic freedom to do what she wants to do since she is the teacher. While the English Department Chairperson understands Ms. Jones' arguments, Ms. Jones agrees that there are not only social and cultural mores that should be respected, but also legal issues that should not be overlooked--such as not showing other than copyrighted videos that are available in the audio-visual center in Naples. Ms. Jones even acknowledges the fact that the legal issue is a valid one but still professes that she should not have to stick to the basics "because the student population is easily bored and many ninth and tenth graders are dropping out of school to work in the tomato and watermelon fields because they cannot relate to the curriculum." After hearing Ms. Jones' reasoning and arguments for the use/significance of the video, the English Department Chairperson cannot help but agree with Ms. Jones.

Finally, the Department Chair and Ms. Jones meet with the principal, asking for his support. Meanwhile, there is more pressure from the community to fire, or at the very least, not re-employ Ms. Jones. What should the principal do?

What is pre-service candidates' analysis of the case? How does their analysis compare with that of the school faculty analysis which follows?

School Faculty Analysis: Case 1

Carol Bregman, Rebecca Francis, Cynthia Lasky, Mariologa Lebredo, Bertha Moro, Judy Newman, Doris Olesky, Mickey Weiner

The above teachers from Miami-Dade County Public Schools, one of whom is a National Board certified teacher, formed a learning community in the spring and summer of 2000 and spent many hours in a collaborative endeavor vis-à-vis case analyses. Here is the group's analysis of Case 1.

Case Analysis

Step 1: Elements of the Problem

The school faculty concludes from its dialogue that the elements in this case are as follows: (a) how much academic freedom or poetic license does a teacher have in the use of curriculum materials? (b) should parents exert any influence over staffing or evaluation practices in schools? and (c) open communication vis-a-vis schools and parents and the balance between school administrations having an open door policy to listen to parents *and* being supportive of teachers.

Step 2: Identifying the Facts in the case

The group sees the following facts in the case:

1. The high school is in a rural area with a diverse population.
2. The community is predominated by an ultra-conservative population.
3. The community is predominated by an ultra-conservative population.
4. Parents wish to maintain a conservative community.
5. Racial discrimination and drugs are present.
6. The principal is confronted by a parent with a complaint about the new English teacher.
7. This parent is also a member of the school board.

8. The parent wants the English teacher fired for showing a music video in class.
9. The principal speaks to the English department chair who has 18 years of experience.
10. The English department chair confers with the new teacher (Ms. Jones) and lets her know that a parent is upset about the music video shown in class.
11. Ms. Jones admits to showing many videos in class, most of which are a part of an approved curriculum. She also admits to showing a music video, Thriller, which is not part of the approved curriculum.
12. The department chair and Ms. Jones meet with the principal and ask for his support.

Step 3: Understanding the Problem

The group identifies the following issues as having a bearing on the case even though they are not stated explicitly in the case:

1. What authority do school board members have? Is a principal evaluation impacted by school board members in any way? If there are cases in which a principal employment status or work location has been influenced by a school board member, then perhaps the principal decisions are impacted due to fear or political pressure.
2. Can a teacher be fired based upon school board or parent recommendation? What are the procedures for evaluating teachers performance? If there are cases in which a principal evaluation has been influenced by a school board member, then it may be more likely that a school board member complaint about a teacher or teacher behavior is acknowledged.
3. To what ethnic/religious/political groups do the principal, Ms. Jones and the school board members belong? If there is a pattern, such as a parent only complaining about certain teachers, or a principal only receiving complaints from certain parents and not a random sampling from the school community, perhaps these factors are in some way linked with attitudes or behavior.
4. Has the parent criticized Ms. Jones or other faculty members before? There may be a pattern if the same parent continues to complain about the same teacher, or a group of teachers.

5. Knowing whether this has been a recurring pattern or an isolated complaint may be useful to see whether the problem is with a teacher or a behavior, for example.

6. Has the parent had a conference with Ms. Jones prior to this incident? On how many occasions and what was the tone? It may be useful to know if the parent has tried to solve the problem or at least communicate with the teacher prior to visiting the principal so that we know, for instance, if the parent is trying to understand the situation or judge the situation without background knowledge.

7. Is Ms. Jones a first-year teacher? Is she new to the profession, district or school? If a teacher is new to a school or community, decisions might be made with less breadth or depth of knowledge and certain school policies, for example, may be unfamiliar.

8. Where did Ms. Jones obtain the music video? If it was obtained from the school district audio-visual library then it may be approved to be shown. It if was brought in from home, then maybe a different set of rules exists for teachers to follow before showing videos which are not on the approved list.

9. Is Ms. Jones aware of the school or district policy for showing videos? Was the video documented in her lesson plans? If she is aware of a policy and did not follow it, perhaps an error in judgement occurred.

10. Was there a purpose for showing the video? Was the purpose communicated to the students before watching the video? Was there a follow-up assignment to the video? Were the curriculum goals of the lesson met? Does the teacher have any work samples which reference the video and offer evidence that the video enhanced the goals of the unit? A clear justification for selecting and showing this music video may be stated and supported by learning outcomes so that the video use cannot be perceived as random or haphazard, but instead, as sound professional judgement.

11. Has the parent making the complaint ever watched the video? This may reveal whether or not the parent was attacking the artist who made the video or the content contained in the video. Also, one would be able to know which part(s) of the video the parent(s) found objectionable and why.

12. Who checks lesson plans? It would be helpful to know if there is a mentor, coach, or department chair who is in part responsible for assisting new teachers in an understanding of the school policies.
13. Has Ms. Jones received satisfactory evaluations by the principal and supervising staff prior to this incident? If her past performance indicates that she is a competent decision maker, perhaps this complaint is less significant then if there has been a history of incompetence or errant judgement.
14. Is Ms. Jones a member of a teachers union or other professional organizations? If she is feeling harassed or unsupported, she can receive advice from colleagues. Also, if she is a member of a professional organization, she may be accepting her responsibility for her own personal and professional development by networking and collaborating with others who may have had a similar experience.

Step 3: Relevant Knowledge Base

The group notes that answers to the foregoing issues is predicated upon one having a sound knowledge (theoretical, empirical, craft wisdom, content) of the following concepts/ideas, etc:

- Educational governance of schools.
- Teacher rights.
- Teacher evaluation.
- Ethnic group relations.
- School policy regarding parents' feedback of classroom instruction.
- Teacher and parent conferences.
- First-year teaching.
- School policy regarding the use of media.
- Assessing student learning.
- Induction programs for beginning teachers.
- Membership in teacher professional organizations and unions.

Step 4: Finding Assumptions

The school faculty sees the following taken for granted in the case, and identifies those assumptions that may be invalid based on evidence in the case or on current professional knowledge:

- Videos are used as instructional resources to supplement and enhance the curriculum. The group feels that current school realities provide validity for this assumption.
- Certain videos are a part of the *approved* curriculum while others are not. The group sees the evidence in the case as pointing to the validity of this assumption.
- Music videos should be used to modernize and update the standard curriculum. The group finds the beginning teacher in the case holding to this assumption which according to the group's professional knowledge is a valid assumption.
- Teachers can choose materials to enhance their curriculum. Based on professional knowledge, the group finds this to be a valid assumption.
- There are multiple ways of teaching and learning. The group maintains that current knowledge on teaching and learning affirms the validity of this assumption.
- Connecting to students interests can increase engagement and/or learning. The group maintains that current knowledge on teaching and learning affirms the validity of this assumption.
- Teachers have a responsibility to know the community in which they teach. The group maintains that current knowledge on teaching and learning affirms the validity of this assumption.
- If a student watches a video, it will influence his/her behavior. The group finds this assumption to be invalid. Empirical evidence suggests that some students behavior may be influenced, but not necessarily all students.
- The parent complaining about the video did not confer with Ms. Jones prior to discussing the matter with the principal. The group finds the evidence in the case as supporting the validity of this assumption.
- Principals are supportive of teachers. The group finds that some principals are supportive of teachers but it is not an absolute that all principals are supportive of teachers. Hence, the group finds this assumption to be valid in some cases and invalid in others.

- School board members influence principals and staffing decisions. The group feels the assumption is valid given current schooling realities. On the other hand, the group feels that if influence borders on manipulation then it should not be taken for granted.

Step 5: Detecting Arguments

The group identified the following arguments in the case; arguments held by characters in the case or imbedded in some decision. The group, however, finds errors in reasoning in each of the arguments:

- The moral fabric of children can be ruined by watching certain videos. The children in Ms. Jones class watched the music video Thriller, therefore the moral fabric of the children will be ruined. The group finds the informal fallacy of *non-sequitur* in this argument.
- If a video is not part of the assigned curriculum then it should not be shown. The music video Thriller was not part of the assigned curriculum, therefore it should not have been shown. The group finds that this argument *begs the question* vis-a-vis the use of professional judgment.
- Ghost stories have been seen by students and parents before the music video. Thriller is a ghost story, therefore Thriller can be shown to students. The group finds that this argument *begs the question* regarding differences of degree and kind.
- If I have academic freedom then I should be allowed to do what I want. Teachers have academic freedom and I am a teacher, therefore I should be allowed to show the music video Thriller. The group notes that while it is generally true that academic freedom does provide certain latitude in the pursuit of knowledge, that one cannot apply the principle indiscriminately to each and every situation (the informal fallacy of *division*).
- School board members have authority in staffing decisions regarding teachers. I am a member of the school board and Ms. Jones is a teacher, therefore I have authority to fire Ms. Jones.

The group notes a disconnect between the conclusion and the reason offered for the conclusion and therefore sees an error in reason here (*does not follow - non-sequitur*).

- When students can relate to the curriculum, learning is improved. Students relate to music videos, therefore music videos can improve learning. The group notes that a causal connection is being made in the argument, that is, that something precedes another thing which is therefore caused by the antecedent thing - the error of *post hoc fallacy*.

Step 6: Interpretation of Case

The case centers around a new English teacher who chooses to supplement the English curriculum and use a music video in her poetry unit. However, the music video she selected did not seem appropriate to a complaining parent. Issues such as how to make a curriculum relevant to lives of students, as well as policies and procedures for acquiring approved videos and curriculum resources are inherent in the case.

Teachers make decisions as to which resources are most appropriate to meet the needs of learners and the curriculum. However, the critical question is how much academic freedom or poetic license does a teacher have? How much input should students or teachers have when choosing resources or projects to be used within a unit or curriculum? It is not clear that the parent, school board member, the English Department Chair or the teacher Ms. Jones is cognizant of legal precedent regarding whether academic freedom protects the assignment of controversial materials. Courts have ruled that academic freedom does protect the assignment of controversial materials if the material is relevant to the subject, is appropriate to the age and maturity of the students, and does not cause disruption (*Parducci v. Rutland*, 316 F. Supp. 352 N.D.Ala. 1970). On the other hand, legal precedent also shows that academic freedom does not allow teachers to disregard the text and syllabus (*Clark v. Holmes*, 474 F. @d 928 8th Cir. 1972, *cert. denied*, 411 U.S. 972 1973).

According to Fischer et al. (1999) "All parental objections to curriculum and instruction are based on two conflicting propositions. The first asserts that parents have the right to guide the upbringing of their children.

The second proclaims that states and boards of education have the power to make and enforce reasonable regulations for the efficient and effective conduct of schools" (443).

Are there strong moral grounds for the parent's objection to the use of the music video in this case? Should reference by a parent to satanic influence be used as the justification to remove curriculum materials? If the materials are not "subversive" or "maliciously written" then local school boards have discretion in the choice of curriculum materials. So the school board's and school's policies regarding the use of supplementary materials is critical to this case.

Nothing in the case suggests that the principal and department chair are clear about the district's policy regarding non-State adopted books and other instructional materials. For example, Miami-Dade County School Board Rules indicate: "Procedures shall be established to provide for evaluation and selection of non-State adopted books and other materials needed to pursue the objectives of a school, region, or district-wide program. Such procedures and guidelines shall permit the individual school, region, or district staff to assume responsibility for the selection. Final authority for the review and selection of materials at the school level shall be vested in the administrative head, the principal; at the regional level in the Superintendent for Region Operations; and at the district level, in the Assistant Superintendent for Elementary and Secondary Education" (School Board Rule 6Gx13-6A-1.26 in Miami-Dade County Public Schools' Staff Handbook).

It is also not clear whether the parent and school member are aware that school policy dictates the criteria to evaluate instructional materials and educational media and the procedures for consideration of protests concerning instructional materials and educational media. Again for example, the Miami-Dade School Board Rules state that "Any citizen may file a complaint with a school or the district concerning the use of particular curriculum materials, textbooks and ancillary items, library books, and non-print media. Challenged materials may be removed from use only after the following informal and formal due process procedures have been completed" (Miami-Dade County Public School's Staff Handbook). It seems that the parent and school member is asking for the dismissal of a teacher without due process.

In the area of parental involvement, should parents exert any influence over staffing or evaluation practices? Since the dissatisfied parent happened to be a school board member, issues of power and politics are also a part of this scenario.

Should not the school board member be cognizant of the processes for evaluating teachers and the grounds for dismissal of tenured teachers only for "cause" - insubordination, incompetency, immorality, and unprofessional conduct? Does the use of the video constitute any of these grounds?

Sometimes open communication can prevent problems, such as parents being aware of the curriculum as well as some of the resources which will be used.

However, when a conflict arises, for example, between a parent and teacher, what is the sequence of events which should precede a conference between a principal and a parent? The balance between having an open-door policy to listen to parents *and* being supportive of teachers is a concern.

It seems that the principal should be in a position to remind the parent of relevant school and district policies, and therefore help to clarify the distinction between lending an ear to an individual's concern and making sure that actions taken are guided by sound professional judgment and adherence to school and district policies.

Solution(s)

- Each fall, the school or the English department can hold a curriculum fair, at which time course goals and materials are shared with parents and school board members. Teachers at this time have an opportunity to meet members of the community as well as family members of their students and thereby explain their courses, selection of materials and the school mission. Parents have opportunities to express concerns. This meeting can be practice in setting a positive school climate for the remainder of the year. Any parents or families who cannot attend can be contacted and invited to come to school at an alternate time and day.
- Veteran teachers can volunteer to mentor new teachers so that school and district policies and procedures become familiar. In addition, each staff member may put together a professional development team consisting of other teachers who will collaborate and work together throughout the year. On occasion, parents could be invited to team planning meetings.

- When a problem arises between a teacher and a parent, a policy is adopted by the administration that requires the parent to first meet with the teacher before bringing the problem to the office. Subsequent to this parent/teacher conference, all parties (principal, parent and teacher) can meet together to discuss the situation and its resolution.

Case 2

Mrs. Mann was in the process of giving a morning reading lesson when Eric came up to the table crying, "Mrs. Mann, Michael hit me!"

Mrs. Mann glanced up and saw Michael standing with his fists clenched and a scowl upon his face. She asked Mary to be the teacher while she went over and talked to Michael.

"Michael," Mrs. Mann began, "why did you hit Eric?"

"Because I wanted to," Michael blurted out.

"Well, Michael," she said, "you know that because of your behavior you won't have your computer time today."

Michael just stared at her and said nothing. Mrs. Mann had dealt with problems with Michael before. He had a propensity for hitting his classmates without provocation. This tendency was becoming more and more pronounced. Being punished by the principal, and assertive discipline techniques were not working anymore. Michael would just become sullen and refuse to participate in class activities.

Later that afternoon, the class has dispersed into centers. Mrs. Mann was circling the room monitoring the students. She came upon Michael, who was sitting with his back to her at the art center. She peered over Michael's shoulder. Michael had made a casket-like object made of clay.

"Michael, what are you making?" she inquired.

"See this," Michael responded, as he opened the casket-like object, and pointed to the figure inside, "That's you in there. You're dead."

A feeling of fear crept up Mrs. Mann's spine. Michael needed help that she could no longer provide. During her PE break, Mrs. Mann called Michael's grandparents and asked them to come in for a conference the following morning.

Mrs. Mann began the conference by expressing her concern for Michael.

"Michael has exhibited some behavioral patterns that disturb the class," Mrs. Mann informed the grandparents.

"What did he do now?" they asked.

"Well, he hits other children without provocation. He made a clay figure that looked like a casket and said that I was dead in there. Other disciplinary measures are just not working," Mrs. Mann said.

"Michael had a difficult childhood," his grandmother explained. "His mother left him with me in Puerto Rico when she married an American man from Tennessee. He hasn't seen much of her. He calls me "mama" and his mother "sister.""

"We have a very good Guidance Committee that deals with students' problems. If you agree, I could refer Michael to them," added Mrs. Mann.

At the end of the conference, the grandparents agreed to turn over the matter of Michael's behavior to the Guidance Committee for further evaluation. Mrs. Mann felt good about the conference. Michael would finally get the help he needed.

A week later, Dr. Mayfield, the county school psychologist, came to observe Michael. Mrs. Mann conducted her class as usual. From the back of the classroom came a loud commotion.

"Move over! I want a drink of water!" Michael ordered. The boy in front of Michael fell down and exclaimed, "Mrs. Mann, Michael pushed me!"

"Michael, why did you push him?" asked Mrs. Mann.

"Cause I was thirsty and he was in my way," Michael reported.

"Michael, you know you must wait your turn like everyone else. Being polite is important. You must have good manners in order to have friends," reasoned Mrs. Mann.

"I don't want any friends," Michael barked.

"I'll be your friend, Michael, and come over to your house to play," offered Ronnie.

"If you come over to my house, I'll cut you up into little pieces with my machete," threatened Michael.

Ronnie backed off. Michael returned to his seat to complete his work.

At the end of the day, Mrs. Mann asked Dr. Mayfield what he thought of Michael's behavior. Dr. Mayfield swallowed hard and answered, "Well, I thought Michael's behavior was normal for an Hispanic child. They usually are aggressive."

Mrs. Mann felt she had been slapped in the face. She was accustomed to having Hispanic students in her class. Mrs. Mann knew that Michael's behavior was inappropriate for any child regardless of where he or she might come from. She thought she would call the grandparents in for another conference.

Once again Mrs. Mann expressed her concern for Michael. She suggested that maybe Michael had an emotional problem.

"What!" the grandmother exclaimed, "Michael has no such problem. He just needs more discipline."

Mrs. Mann left the conference wondering what she was going to do. The grandparents didn't want to acknowledge the fact that Michael's problem might be emotionally based. The school psychologist was a big disappointment. The thought crept into her mind, "How will I teach the remainder of the year and deal with Michael's behavior?"

As she was leaving that day, Mrs. Mann made up her mind to try to present Michael's case to the Guidance Committee once again. This time she would be prepared.

What is pre-service candidates' analysis of the case? How does their analysis compare with that of the school faculty analysis which follows?

School Faculty Analysis: Case 2

Carol Bregman, Rebecca Francis, Cynthia Lasky, Mariolga Lebredo, Bertha Moro, Judy Newman, Doris Olesky, Mickey Weiner

Case Analysis

Step 1: Elements of the Problem

The school faculty concludes from its dialogue that the elements in this case are as follows: (a) what strategies/resources are available to help teachers assist students who repeatedly misbehave? (b) when a teacher observes that a child needs help beyond what is provided by a classroom teacher, how can appropriate resources best be obtained? and (c) what types of support from the school and/or community are available to help families and teachers collaborate to help children?

Step 2: Identifying the Facts in the Case

According to the school faculty, the following are the facts in the case:

1. The teacher has dealt with problems with Michael's behavior before.
2. Michael has been sent to the office where he was paddled by the principal.
3. Michael made a clay casket at the art center in the classroom and told Mrs. Mann the figure inside was her, dead.
4. Mrs. Mann called Michael's grandparents more than once about his behavior.
5. The grandmother told Mrs. Mann that Michael had a difficult childhood.
6. Mrs. Mann referred Michael to the school's guidance committee.
7. Michael threatened Ronnie, another student in the classroom.
8. Michael's grandparents admitted that he needed special help with his behavior.

9. Michael's grandmother did not want to agree with Mrs. Mann that Michael may have an emotional problem.

Step 3: Understanding the Problem

The school faculty notes that the following have a bearing on the case:

1. Have other teachers had behavior problems with Michael?. Does his behavior improve or worsen at certain times in the day or during certain academic subjects? If other teachers have had similar problems with Michael this may establish a pattern and the teacher may be able to get support and assistance from these other teachers in resolving the problem. A review of Michael's cumulative record could also provide important information on his background.
2. What grade level does this problem involve? An incident of a child making a casket out of clay may not be of concern if the child is in pre-K or kindergarten, but it may be of concern if the child is older. It may indicate emotional problems and a tendency towards violence.
3. Has Michael been in school before - is this his first year at the school? If it is his first year at the school, he may not have made friends or developed appropriate social skills to interact with others. If Michael has never been in a school environment before, he may be having trouble adjusting to the classroom setting, which would be quite different than his home setting.
4. Where is this school located? The geographic location of the school may be important in determining ethnic make-up and cultural identity of the community. If the school is primarily Hispanic there should be resources and Hispanic staff available to assist in bridging cultural awareness and understanding.
5. Is Michael the only child in the home - if there are siblings, have they also been behavior problems? If Michael is an only child and is receiving a lot of attention at home, this may be an explanation for his having trouble adjusting to a classroom where the teacher has a number of students to whom she pays attention.

If there are siblings in the home that exhibit similar problems at school, one may want to look at the home environment and its effect on the children.

6. Has there been a history of alcohol, drug or physical abuse in this family? A history of such problems may influence Michael's behavioral/emotional problems. It is important to know if there are such problems if the family is undergoing counseling or some type of treatment. Physical abuse within the family may play a role in Michael's aggression towards others.

7. Who are the members of the guidance committee? Experienced teachers, new teachers and the counselor should be members of this committee, along with the principal and any other administrative staff.

8. What is the process used by the guidance committee to assist and evaluate referrals? Here it is essential to know what the steps are that a teacher needs to follow to refer a student, and what paperwork, documentation and other information is necessary for referrals.

Step 3: Relevant Knowledge Base

The group states that answers to the foregoing may be obtained through one's knowledge of the following topics/ideas:

- School district policy for referring children to the guidance team.
- Teachers' Union policy on maintaining classroom climate conducive for teaching and learning.
- Peer collaboration/collegial support.
- Knowledge of child development.
- Curriculum which addresses the needs of the whole child.
- Teacher and parent conferences/family involvement.
- Social case-history of child/family.
- Student profile/data from school records.
- Resources available to help students, teachers and families identify and understand the needs of the child.

Step 4: Finding Assumptions

The group notes the following things taken for granted in the case and identifies their validity or invalidity:

- When a teacher's attempts to correct misbehavior fail, administrative support may be sought. The group finds current school policy provides validity for this assumption.
- Families can help teachers help students with academic, behavioral or emotional concerns when open communication and family involvement occur between home and school. The group finds this assumption to be valid only if trust is established between home and school.
- Situations that occur in a child's home may have an impact on a child's emotions and behavior at school. The group maintains that current knowledge on teaching and learning affirms the validity of this assumption.
- The guidance committee and a school psychologist will listen to a teacher's concerns regarding students in the classroom and offer insights as to how to help students. The group finds this assumption to be valid when unbiased and professional opinions are offered, and invalid in cases such as this one, where Dr. Mayfield expects Hispanic children to be aggressive.
- Teachers meet with parents/guardians when a behavior problem with a student persists. The group finds that current school policy provides validity for this assumption.
- School and community resources exist so that a child who is having severe behavioral problems can receive help. Based on professional knowledge, the group finds this assumption to be valid when the proper resources are connected to those in need of assistance.

Step 5: Detecting Arguments

The following arguments are held by characters in the case or imbedded in some decision. Errors in reasoning are noted by the school faculty:

- Hispanic students are usually aggressive in their behavior. Michael is an Hispanic child, therefore, aggressive behavior in school is normal for him. The group finds this argument to be circular, and devoid of any corroborating evidence.

- If the county's school psychologist feels Michael's behavior is normal, then his behavior must be normal. The guidance committee's job is to help evaluate students who teachers feel have severe behavioral problems, therefore, they should assist the teacher in finding appropriate resources to assist a child. The group finds this argument to contain an appeal to authority and devoid of corroborative evidence.
- Mrs. Mann has had several problems with Michael's behavior in the classroom and has tried various disciplinary techniques which have been unsuccessful, therefore, she needs to seek outside resources to help Michael. The group finds this to be a valid argument if no equivocation is intended in the use of "outside resources."
- Michael's mother left him and he refers to her as "sister", therefore, Michael has been affected by this emotionally and this may be the root of his anger. The group feels that this argument begs the question regarding Michael's emotional state.
- The guidance committee requires certain documentation and paperwork when referring a case and Mrs. Mann seemed not to have been adequately prepared, therefore, they were not able to assist Michael, properly. This argument does not follow in the group's judgment.

Step 6: Interpretation of Case

This case involves a student, Michael, who repeatedly misbehaves, breaks classroom rules and acts aggressively toward other students. His teacher has tried various measures to get Michael the help she feels he needs and deserves, yet her attempts have up to this point not proven successful. He continues to act out and she continues to feel frustrated and defeated since Michael's problems disrupt his learning as well as the learning environment of the entire class.

Classroom teachers are responsible for the safety and well-being of all students in their classrooms. When a student's behavior threatens the safety of him/herself or others in the classroom, teachers have a responsibility to do what needs to be done in order to maintain a safe and positive learning environment for all learners. Moreover, "Teachers have the authority to remove a seriously disruptive student from the classroom...."

This authority is vested in the Contract between United Teachers of Dade and Miami-Dade County Public School System (Article VII, p.17). In this case, however, Mrs. Mann is faced with a dilemma, for if and when she removes Michael from her classroom, not only is his own learning interrupted but the assertive discipline and paddling used by the administration thus far have not seemed to be effective in helping Michael improve his self-control and classroom conduct. If we agree that the administration and guidance teams have a responsibility to lend support to teachers and students when continuous disruptive behaviors occur in the classrooms, we would want to know what types of support, if any, have been tried beyond assertive discipline and paddling. Has anyone tried to talk to Michael privately; find a mentor or listener for him; invite him to join the art club? In addition, what sorts of strategies has Mrs. Mann tried beyond telephoning his family on two separate occasions? Has she incorporated any conflict resolution or peer mediation into her daily or weekly routine? Nevertheless, it would seem beneficial for a collaborative effort to ensue in order to try to solve this problem. Perhaps a collectivity of teachers and professionals who are in some way connected to Michael or Mrs. Mann could collaborate, as suggested by Birman et al (2000), in order to develop a common understanding of the problem and solution.

When Mrs. Mann spoke to members of Michael's family, they seemed to be receptive to the idea that Michael needed help as long as they understood his problem to be behavioral. When it was suggested that Michael's emotions may be a part of the problem, the family's reaction became negative.

Educators can help family members understand that when a child needs help, it matters not whether the cause is academic, behavioral, emotional, psychological, or a combination of factors. Why is one type of problem perceived as more or less honorable, tolerable or traumatic than any other? Schools that address the needs of the whole child, academic, social, emotional, etc., are helping to foster not only cognitive ideals but also mentally healthy children. Promoting an understanding in Michael's family and all of Mrs. Mann's students that feelings and emotions are natural for all human beings and worthy of being addressed inside the classroom can help debunk the myths that academics are the only important aspect of the curriculum and that to be intelligent means only that one must score well on standardized tests.

According to Goleman (1995), attention to more than academics must be fostered in classrooms so that children are given opportunities to become emotionally literate and learn about becoming more self-aware, cooperative, empathetic, and socially adept.

Solution(s)

- Mrs. Mann can request that a visiting teacher or counselor visit Michael's home to get a feel for the conditions in which he is living, and develop better communication between the home and the school.
- Mrs. Mann can invite Michael's grandparents to visit the classroom or volunteer in the school. This could serve to open communication between home and school even further.
- An administrator needs to be in the child-study team meeting when a teacher refers a case to the guidance committee. The guidance committee needs to provide written follow-up and an evaluation to the teacher and principal which illuminates a variety of strategies which have been or are recommended to be tried.
- A teacher must have a clear understanding of expectations required by the guidance committee when referring a case. Also, the teacher, in conjunction with the guidance team, must be willing to look at other strategies or outside resources for assistance as needed. Perhaps if the word "team" is emphasized, at which time guidance and counseling professionals, teachers, administrators, family members and students when appropriate, collaborate to discuss the child's strengths as well as weaknesses, a more comprehensive and longer lasting solution can be achieved.
- The district's and school's curriculum must look beyond merely cognitive objectives and must include a range of programs available to help teachers help students deal with feelings, emotions, crisis or stress. These programs need not be commercially prepared and can be as simple as journal writing or having a group discussion which focuses on self-awareness or getting along with others, for example.

Case 3

Sherry has taught the sixth grade in a northern Florida school for six years. One of her students, Joe, has presented Sherry with a problem with which she has struggled for several months and she is undecided as to what to do about it. Joe does not fit in with the other students either academically or socially. He is a tall, extremely slim youth with a long sad face that is prone to acute acne. He is absent from class quite often and when he attends class he usually appears to be paying very little attention to what is going on. His school work is well below average and he is failing in several areas. He has repeated one grade, and his records indicate that he has always had trouble keeping up with the rest of the students. His standardized test scores indicate that he is slightly below the "normal" range in abilities but his grades are far lower than that. He is always alone and does not interact with the other students either in or out of class. He does not participate in any outside activities and does not appear to have any friends.

Sherry decided that she should do something to help Joe to reach his potential which she believed to be much higher than the circumstances dictated. She had noticed that Joe often did better in math than in other areas, although his math grades were still below average. Sherry thought that unless Joe was somehow motivated to want to learn that he would eventually be a dropout and ruin whatever chances that he might have for success.

Sherry: "Joe, are you having any problems understanding the work assignments?"

Joe: "Naw, just doing the best that I can."

Sherry: "Do you think you can do better?"

Joe: "No, it's the best I can do."

Sherry: "You do better in math than other subjects, do you like math?"

Joe: "Yea, I can use it to figure my pay check when I get a job."

Sherry sent Joe to the appropriate counselors for further testing and the test results were normal. Joe's abilities were sufficient to at least achieve average grades. She consulted with Joe's other teachers who appeared to be interested in Joe but also seemed to be resigned to the fact that Joe was only going to "get by" at the best. One teacher, Glenda, gave Sherry the following information.

Sherry: "Glenda, you have had Joe in several of your classes, did you do anything to help him to improve his grades?"

Glenda: "I tried but he did not respond. I gave him a lot of attention, praised him and gave him work that I thought he could do. He did not respond and after several more attempts to help him I just gave up and decided that the best that I could do was to help him to learn enough to be promoted to the next grade."

Sherry was not satisfied and she decided to learn as much as possible about Joe's home environment. She began to ask Joe questions whenever the opportunity presented itself and she slowly began to piece his home life together. She also talked to other teachers and some of her friends who gave her information concerning Joe's family. Joe was one of six children, two of whom were mentally handicapped. Joe's father was a night watchman and barely made enough money to keep the family going. His mother was an obese woman who had varied illnesses, and was unable to work, and often was too sick to do the housework.

Sherry: "Joe, how many brothers and sisters do you have?"

Joe: "Five, but two of them are handicapped."

Sherry: "What does your father do?"

Joe: "He's a night watchman."

Sherry: "Do you want to be a night watchman too?"

Joe: "Yea, my father does it and he does OK. I help by looking after my brothers and sisters and helping my mom do the housework."

Sherry: "Is your mom sick?"

Joe: "Yea, she is pretty sick because she is so fat and can't get around much. She has heart trouble and a lot of other things."

Sherry: "Do your parents help you with your homework?"

Joe: "Are you kidding? They don't know how to do that stuff."

Sherry: "Do you show them your report cards?"

Joe: "Sure, they sign them and don't say nothing."

Sherry was still convinced that she could help Joe to see that education was valuable and that he had the ability to do better work. Sherry thought that Joe lacked self-confidence and had resigned himself to the fact that poor people just did not have the same opportunities as other people. Joe had alienated himself so that the outside world could not hurt him. Sherry began to formulate a plan that would bolster Joe's self-confidence and improve his self-image. Sherry had read a considerable amount of literature concerning the isolation and alienation that poor and "minority" students experience.

And she thought that Joe's previous teachers had not expected Joe to perform well. As a result, Joe had simply done what was expected of him, he met teacher expectations. Sherry began to ask Joe questions that she thought he could answer:

Sherry: "Joe, what do you think that life was like for the Pilgrims who came to the New World?"

Joe: "It was pretty tough. They didn't have no electricity or air conditioning and the food was bad."

Sherry: "And do you think that you would have liked living during those years?"

Joe: "Maybe, you didn't have to go to school and you could hunt and shoot."

Sherry praised his right answers to questions and ignored his wrong ones. She talked to him outside of class, and simply tried to let him know that she was truly interested in his well-being. After several weeks, Joe actually voluntarily answered a question in class, and his math scores slightly improved. Overall, he was still performing below average but there was a slight improvement. Sherry thought about contacting his parents at this point but decided not to because she thought that they would not understand or care about Joe's school work.

Sherry was determined to continue to help Joe improve but was undecided as to what to do next. She could continue with the present program or she could try to find other methods to help him. She thought that the praise and show of interest should be continued, but she realized that this might not be sufficient to help Joe reach his potential abilities. She wanted to find a way to not only help Joe academically, but also to help him become involved with his fellow students. She thought about forming groups in class and making Joe the spokesman for his group, but she feared that this might frighten Joe, and make his shyness even acute. She also considered asking Joe to help her with a project so that he might later try to persuade other students to help him with the project. Sherry thought that she had to be careful because she was dealing with an under-privileged student who was sensitive to any criticism or possibility of embarrassment. Sherry thought that her determination to help Joe was the right thing to do, but realized that she needed more information, and help from other people.

What is pre-service candidates' analysis of the case? How does their analysis compare with that of the school faculty analysis which follows?

School Faculty Analysis: Case 3

Carol Bregman, Rebecca Francis, Cynthia Lasky, Mariolga Lebredo, Bertha Moro, Judy Newman, Doris Olesky, Mickey Weiner

Case Analysis

Step 1: Elements of the Problem

The school faculty suggests that the major elements in the case are as follows: (a) what happens when a teacher's expectations exceed a student's motivation in terms of academic performance? (b) do students who perform low academically have more difficulty in adulthood? and (c) what impact, if any, do factors related to ethnicity, socioeconomic status and/or family background have on one's academic performance?

Step 2: Identifying the Facts in the Case

The following facts were identified by the school faculty:

1. Joe is one of Sherry's sixth grade students.
2. Joe is absent often from class and has repeated a grade.
3. Joe's standardized test scores are slightly below normal and his grades are far lower than his test scores.
4. Joe often does better in math than in other areas.
5. Sherry has consulted with Joe's other teachers in order to try to understand how best to motivate him yet she has not contacted his parents.
6. Joe's father is a watchman and his mother is obese and suffers from a variety of illnesses.

Step 3: Understanding the Problem

The group identifies the following as having some relationship to the case:

1. How often is Joe absent? What are the reasons for his absences? Joe could be ill or he could be staying home to help his mother. If Joe is ill, the teacher can recommend a physical. If he is staying home to help his mom, maybe the school can get social services to help her.
2. Why was he retained? Absences, grades or both? In what grade was he retained?
3. Has Sherry read the cumulative records for a social history? Has any school representative visited the school? Perhaps she could gain a greater insight into Joe and his situation.
4. What are Joe's academic strengths and talents? This might allow the teacher to determine how best to use his strengths to build upon his weaknesses.
5. Why does Joe do better in math? If it is because he finds it useful, maybe the relevance of other subjects in the curriculum can be explored.

Step 3: Relevant Knowledge Base

The group states that answers to the foregoing may be obtained through one's knowledge of the following topics/ideas:

*   Student case history /family background.
*   Parent conferences.
*   Measures of student achievement /alternative assessment.
*   Project approach for a more holistic curriculum.
*   Relevance in curriculum.
*   Teacher vs. student expectations.
*   Motivation and learning.

Step 4: Finding Assumptions

The school faculty identifies the following things taken for granted:

*   Joe has a difficult home life. The group finds this assumption to be invalid since we are unsure what Joe's perceptions of his home life are.

- Joe lacks self-confidence due to his family situation.
  The group finds this assumption to be invalid since it is not clear
  (a) when and if Joe does lack self-confidence and (b) what the
  cause(s) of his possible lack of confidence might be.
- Sherry believes she can help Joe by getting to know him better.
  The group agrees with the assumption that often times when
  teachers take time to get to know students, there can be positive
  outcomes.
- Because Joe comes from a poor family, he has academic
  hardships. The group finds this assumption to be invalid based
  on professional experiences which find no causal influence
  between socioeconomic factors and academic performance.

Step 5: Detecting Arguments

The group identified the following arguments in the case; arguments
held by characters in the case or imbedded in some decision. The
group finds errors in reasoning in some of the arguments:

- Joe comes from a poor, uneducated family, therefore, he does
  not value education. From the group's perspective this argument
  contains a *non-sequitur.*
- Joe's parents are poor and uneducated, therefore, they do not
  take an interest in Joe's progress in school. Again the group sees
  another *non-sequitur* here.
- Joe's mother is ill and obese; therefore, Joe feels he needs to help
  out at home. According to the school faculty, this is an irrelevant
  conclusion.
- Sherry gave Joe praise and extra individual attention; therefore,
  he showed a slight improvement in his performance. The group
  sees a connection between the antecedent praise and the
  consequent of improved performance. It sees nothing fallacious
  in this argument.
- Sherry feels Joe's parents do not care or understand him,
  therefore, they will not help Joe. The group finds a connection
  between not caring and not helping although there are
  circumstances in which a lack of caring does not automatically
  mean a lack of help.
- Joe is under-privileged; therefore, he is sensitive to criticism or
  the possibility of embarrassment. The group finds that this
  argument begs the question regarding the kind of criticism.

Step 6: Interpretation of Case

The case centers around an adolescent boy who the teacher perceives as working below his ability. Sherry, the teacher, has taken up the cause of this young man as her own personal mission. The child, Joe, however, may not need the kind of help Sherry tries to give. She may be looking for a problem that is not really there.

Often, a teacher's expectations for a student exceed a student's own self-expectations or motivation. In this case it appears that Sherry has "diagnosed" Joe's problem without sufficient investigation into his particular case, and all the factors that may be affecting Joe's attitude and performance in school.

A critical question here is despite Joe's family background, socio-economic status and lack of interest in most academic subjects, can he still survive in life and become a productive member of society? It seems clear that Sherry has determined that Joe's lack of motivation in school is a result of his underprivileged background and family circumstances. Yet, Sherry has never visited Joe's home or even spoken to his parents. Even though his family may be poor and uneducated, this does not mean that they do not value and support Joe's education. His parents may feel that Joe should have opportunities that they never had and actually greatly encourage his success in school.

Joe seems to have responsibilities at home in taking care of his younger siblings and assisting his handicapped mother. Through these responsibilities, Joe may feel useful and appreciated. He may have a close relationship with his parents and feel loved, as well as happy at home. If Sherry discussed her concerns with Joe's parents instead of regarding them as inept, unable or unwilling to help him, she may be more successful in her efforts to reach Joe. Sherry may want to ask Joe questions about his life and how he feels. Is he happy at home? Does he feel close to his parents? What does he like to do in his spare time? What does he feel he is good at or what is he interested in? Sherry has not tapped into Joe's talents and interests up to this point, and when she does she may begin to see the motivation and results she is hoping to find. Perhaps if she finds out he has an interest in a certain area, she can encourage him to explore this interest. Together, Sherry and Joe may discover that he has a special gift or talent. For example, Joe may be interested in art or music and become more motivated in school if he has the opportunity to express himself in the art club or chorus at school. Research indicates that when students are exposed or immersed in the arts, their self-esteem increases and they may develop more discipline and become more motivated to achieve academically.

It is evident that Sherry needs to redirect her strategies and approach in assisting Joe with his academic problems in school. Instead of worrying about Joe's lack of academic interest, she may need to focus on his strengths and enhance or broaden her curriculum to meet Joe's needs and provide more meaningful and practical experiences for him. If she is able to see that success is measured by more than a compilation of test scores, she may be helping Joe to find successful experiences outside of strictly an academic world. Nothing in this case indicates that Joe is going to fail in life. The factors that affect Joe's life may be looked at as challenges instead of problems and may help him develop a strong character and firm family values. Many times, obstacles in life cause us to persevere and become more determined to survive. Children surprise us all the time with their resilience and power to overcome seemingly adverse situations (Weiner, 1997).

Solution(s)

- Sherry may wish to continue spending time with Joe to get to know him and his family better. She can visit Joe's home with the counselor and talk with his parents to try to get their support.
- If Sherry decides not to label Joe as "poor and underprivileged," then maybe she would more easily see him as a human being who has a multiplicity of strengths rather than deficits.
- Sherry might give Joe responsibilities in the classroom. This might provide leadership opportunities and improve his self-esteem.
- Sherry can learn to recognize and help her students value success as more than an academic issue. She can also help learners see that although mathematical and linguistic abilities are most often used in standardized tests, many other forms of intelligence exist which can be further developed in each learner. Sherry may wish to focus more on an area in which Joe has a real interest and help him develop skills in that area; everyone

has a gift or talent. She might also wish to focus on helping Joe get to know himself better by exploring different kinds of class projects which incorporate skills that Joe and the other students find relevant and meaningful.

- Some students are loners and/or low-achievers academically, but this does not mean they cannot be happy and survive in society or in life.

Case 4

"Pass your papers to the front, please," said Mrs. Blake. A few of her students sighed as the quizzes changed hands and found their way to the first row.

Susan Blake taught a special class at Rolfe Middle School. It was part of a dropout prevention program, and very different from other classes. In addition to having the same group of kids for the entire school day, she used a special system of grading based on effort and attitude, because receiving an "A" meant nothing to these students. They were placed in this class because they were determined to be at high risk for dropping out of school.

When the quiz papers reached Samantha Daniels, who occupied the desk nearest Mrs. Blake's, she noticed something which she found to be very peculiar. Max and Mohammed, the two boys who sat in the back row, had taken a different quiz with less than half as many questions as there had been on everyone else's quiz.

"Hey," said Sam. "What's with this? Max and Mohammed got easier tests."

This complaint made Susan a little nervous. She had not expected this, and she was concerned that the students did not understand the situation. As she searched for the best way to explain, she noticed that the rest of the class was becoming very interested.

"I gave Max and Mohammed a quiz with less questions on it because they need more time to complete their work."

"That ain't fair!" exclaimed Brian.

Susan could see how this would not be fair in a regular classroom, but this was not a regular class. She realized that these children had a tough time fitting in to the rigid structure of school, so she was willing to make adjustments for them. She let them listen to walkmans while they worked provided she had screened and approved the tapes, and she did not say anything if a student called her by her first name.

"It isn't fair," Brian repeated.

Slouching in their back-row desks, Max and Mohammed looked at each other, then at the floor. They felt uncomfortable with all of this attention and wished that everyone would stop talking about them and leave them alone. Neither of them felt like being in school in the first place.

The two boys had very poor attendance records which, Mrs. Blake believed, accounted for their poor reading and mathematics skills. They still counted on their fingers and read on a first grade level. They came from economically handicapped families, and had each been in trouble with the law.

The boys were easily discouraged by school work, and Susan wanted to help. She thought that if they had an amount of work that they could complete, they would gain a sense of accomplishment. She could not let them drown; she believed she was right. Mrs. Blake knew that she was in charge, and that she had the final word, but she felt it important that the children understand.

Katrina joined the discussion. "I don't want so much work neither," she said.

"Trina, you do just fine with your work," explained Mrs. Blake, "but Max and Mohammed aren't ready to do that many problems."

"Forget it! " yelled Mohammed as he pushed his book to the floor. "I won't do none den." He had always been a "bad dude," but now his voice quivered with frustration. He had never liked school, but for the past weeks he had really been trying to do well.

What is pre-service candidates' analysis of the case? How does their analysis compare with that of the school faculty analysis which follows?

School Faculty Analysis: Case 4

Carol Bregman, Rebecca Francis, Cynthia Lasky, Mariolga Lebredo,
Bertha Moro, Judy Newman, Doris Olesky, Mickey Weiner

Case Analysis

Step 1: Elements of the Problem

The school faculty concludes from its dialogue that the elements in
this case are as follows: (a) how should teachers deal with matters of
academic differences and diverse needs of learners in the classroom??
(b) should teachers find and implement the best way to meet the needs
of their students even if those modifications are outside prescribed
curriculum and practices? and (c) is "fair" giving all students the same
curriculum, expectations, goals and instruction; or is "fair" setting
curriculum, expectations, goals and instruction to meet each student's
needs?

Step 2: Identifying the Facts in the Case

The group sees the following facts in the case:

1. Susan Blake teaches a dropout prevention class in a middle
   school.
2. Students were placed in Ms. Blake's class because it was
   determined that they were at high risk for dropping out of school.
3. Ms. Blake used a "special" system to grade students based on
   effort and attitude.
4. Max and Mohammed received tests with less questions than did
   other members in the class.
5. Students in Ms. Blake's class protested that it was "unfair" that
   Max and Mohammed had a different test than they did.
6. Max and Mohammed have poor attendance records, poor reading
   and mathematics skills, come from economically disadvantaged
   families and have been in trouble with the law.

Step 3: Understanding the Problem

The group identifies the following as having a bearing on the case
even though they are not stated explicitly:

1. Did Max and Mohammed realize they were getting a shortened form of the test before they took the test? Did Ms. Blake take their feelings into consideration? If they realized they had a different form of the test and it was explained why, perhaps Max's and Mohammed's reactions to the situation would have been different. They would have been better able to cope with their peer's reactions.

2. How is Ms. Blake's class different from other classes? How are students selected to be in Ms. Blake's class? Knowing the reasons students are selected for the class may explain the need for individualized instruction. It may also explain the class's, Max's and Mohammed's reactions.

3. What is the family life like of both Max and Mohammed? Why were Max and Mohammed in trouble with the law? Knowing the boys' backgrounds may explain their reactions. It may also explain why Ms. Blake decided to modify work for the two boys.

4. How did Ms. Blake decide who got modified tests? Knowing this would address the "fairness" aspect of the problem. It would be a factor in whether the modified tests were really fair. It would also be important when talking to the class about this situation.

5. Are assignments also modified for Max and Mohammed? If they are not, why is there a need to modify the tests? It seems to follow that if there is a need to modify tests for a student than there is a parallel need to modify the same student's daily assignments.

6. How do the other students in the class do academically? Is everyone else in the class on grade level? If Max and Mohammed are the only two students below grade level, it can explain why they are the only two students with modified tests.

7. Do the students in the room know what their dropout prevention label means? If they do not, this may explain all the students' reactions.

8. What are some resources available to Ms. Blake? Are there counseling programs available? Outside resources may help Ms. Blake address the issue of academic differences with her class.

9. Does Ms. Blake hold regular counseling sessions to address the affective needs of her students? If she does, then she may have built a rapport with students to openly discuss the issue of academic differences and "fairness."

10. What exactly is Ms. Blake's "special" grading system? Is it necessary to give tests to support this grading system?

Step 3: Relevant Knowledge Base

The group notes that answers to the forgoing issues is predicated upon one having a sound knowledge (theoretical, empirical craft wisdom, content) of the following concept/ideas, etc.:

- Student labeling.
- Modification of standard curriculum to meet students' needs.
- Policies governing dropout and alternative education.
- Policies governing modifying curriculum.
- Grading policy.
- Motivating reluctant learners.
- Assessment of student learning.
- Teaching to the affective domain and counseling in the classroom.
- Developing a classroom community.
- Using case histories to assess a student's needs.

Step 4: Finding Assumptions

The school faculty sees the following taken for granted in the case, and identifies those assumptions that may be invalid based on evidence in the case or on current professional knowledge:

- All students can learn but they learn in different ways. The group finds this assumption to be valid based on professional knowledge.
- Modifying curriculum is "fair" and appropriate. The group finds this assumption to be valid in cases where modifying the curriculum is based on sound professional judgment and invalid when the curriculum is modified in a random way.
- Dropout prevention and alternative education students may require different teaching methods and curriculum. The group finds that this assumption is valid based on professional experience, and further maintains that there are times that all students may require different teaching methods or curriculum,

regardless of who is labeled dropout prevention or alternative education.

- Teachers may be concerned with both the cognitive and affective aspects of their students. The group finds this assumption to be valid based on professional opinion regarding meeting the needs of the whole child.
- Poor attendance yields poor grades. Better attendance yields better grades. The group finds this assumption to be valid in some cases and not valid in others since professional experience indicates that attendance may be linked, but is not always correlated with earning higher grades.
- It is more likely that academically disadvantaged students will be in a dropout prevention class. The group finds this assumption to be invalid based on professional knowledge and school policy.
- Students in dropout prevention can't do "regular " work. The group's professional expertise suggests that this assumption is invalid since it is not clear exactly what "regular" work is, yet does find validity in stating that there are some forms of work that any of us cannot do without special help or modifications.
- Students in dropout prevention classes are not concerned with their academic performance. Based on professional experience, the group finds this assumption to be too general to be valid for all students.

Step 5: Detecting Arguments

The group identified the following arguments in the case; arguments held by characters in the case or imbedded in some decision. The group, however, finds errors in reasoning in each of the arguments:

- Modifying curriculum to meet the individual needs of students is "fair" and appropriate. Ms. Blake's students have differing needs, therefore, Ms. Blake is fair in modifying students' curriculum. The group notes that the conclusion does not necessarily follow from the premises.
- Teachers of dropout prevention and alternative education should make curricular adaptations. Ms. Blake teaches a dropout prevention class, therefore, she needs to adapt the standard curriculum. This is a valid argument from the group's perspective.

- Teachers need to meet the needs of all students. Each and every student has his/her own needs; therefore, Ms. Blake needs to meet the needs of all her students. The group sees a four-term fallacy in this argument.
- Teachers should deal with the affective domain in their classes. Ms. Blake is a teacher, therefore, she should deal with the affective domain in her class. This argument is valid according to the school faculty.
- Students in dropout prevention classes are placed there because they have had little success in "regular" classes. Max and Mohammed are students in a dropout prevention program, therefore, they were not successful in a "regular" class. The group finds the structure of the argument to be valid, but feels the content of the argument commits the fallacy of *non-sequitur*.
- Students do not like being identified as different or lower achieving to their peers. Max and Mohammed are students, therefore, they did not like being identified as different in front of their peers. The school faculty group finds this argument to be structurally valid but not sound vis-à-vis because it commits the fallacy of *non-sequitur*.

Step 6: Interpretation of Case

As quiz papers were being collected in a middle school alternative education class, a student observed that two other students received a shorter quiz containing fewer questions.

The issue of "fairness" arose as a topic of contention when this discovery was made. The teacher tried to explain that not all students were able to complete the longer version of the test.

At this point, two of the students who received the shorter quiz became frustrated with the attention, while other students in the class were uncomfortable since they felt they were being treated unfairly by being given the longer test.

First of all, one may wish to determine the purpose of Mrs. Blake's assessment before proceeding with a discussion of what is fair. On the one hand, if she is administering a standardized test of any sort, all students receive the same test and test security measures are in effect.

On the other hand, if she is not giving a standardized test, and it appears from elements in this case that she is not but instead is attempting to measure what her students have learned, then it would stand to reason that her assessments could, indeed, be modified to fit the needs of the learners.

It is stated in the case that the teacher uses a special grading system based on effort and attitude because receiving an "A" is meaningless to these students. However, it is not clear who developed this grading system or whether this grading system is school or district approved. According to the Pupil Progression Plan (1999, I-60) of Miami-Dade County Public Schools, this type of grading system is not allowed as academic grades are to reflect the student's academic progress and must not be based upon the student's effort or conduct.

Nevertheless, in this case, was the teacher the person who determined that her students needed a different grading system because her experience with this class indicated they were unmotivated? Was the teacher assuming that students in dropout prevention could not be motivated or were not capable of adhering to a "regular" grading system? Or did the school require the dropout prevention program to use a different sort of grading system? Since these questions may be related to a program's content or teacher expectations, issues of fairness and learner equity arise.

In addition, one wonders if the students (a) were aware of how the grading system being used is different from other grading systems with which they may already be familiar and (b) had any involvement in the development of the grading system.

These questions are of particular interest, for when students work collaboratively with the teacher or other students to help design their own projects, assignments or assessments, motivation may increase as students feel empowered to make decisions that impact their own learning. Since it is not clear which methods, if any, have been tried to motivate students and help them to want to learn, one would want to incorporate as many strategies as possible to get to know each learner, his or her areas of interest, hobbies, talents, expectations, goals, etc., in order to formulate a curriculum which meets learners' needs as it incorporates learners' interests.

Should all students in the same class receive the same curriculum, assessments and evaluations even though learning styles, motivation, skill levels and needs can be dramatically different within and between members of the same class?

Should dropout prevention programs receive special consideration? Since each human being is unique and learns in different ways, teachers have a responsibility to become aware of each student's learning needs and make necessary adjustments to the curriculum in order to address the individual needs of learners (see Professional Assessment & Comprehensive Evaluation System, Miami-Dade County, Florida, 2000). One of the core propositions of the National Board for Professional Teaching Standards maintains that teachers are committed to students and their learning and "recognize individual differences in their students and adjust their practices accordingly" (1997, p.5).

Indeed, there are many ways to differentiate one's curriculum, and Wehrman (2000) contends that teachers may decide to differentiate by modifying the content, process or product. Moreover, differentiating the curriculum is not only a reasonable and wise choice for Ms. Blake and teachers in dropout prevention classes but for teachers in any classroom. According to Pettig (2000), differentiated practice can improve learning for all students as new windows of possibility for teaching and learning can be opened.

Solution(s)

- Ms. Blake might wish to hold some counseling sessions or group discussions to address the issues of academic differences, individual differences and the universality of being human. There are many different techniques that are appropriate to addressing these issues (i.e.. role-playing, bibliotherapy etc.).
- Ms. Blake might invite a counselor to discuss the issues of academic differences and fairness with her class. Perhaps a discussion about labeling, as well as the many sociological, economic and other factors associated with this practice would help students understand how they were selected and placed into this class.
- Before students are placed in a dropout prevention class, the school could be proactive and explain to students what placement in the class means and how it will be differ from a "regular" class.
- As early as the first day of class, Ms. Blake might lead a discussion about how all learners are alike *and* different, as all have individual strengths and talents. She might find it useful in

helping the class to understand that there are many ways to learn and many types of intelligence that can be drawn upon.

- Perhaps by working cooperatively in small groups, the children can begin to see that each person in the class is uniquely diverse, yet a vital and contributing member of the classroom community. Given the multiplicity of preferences and learning styles which may have been identified by working collaboratively in the classroom, Ms. Blake might ask the students to determine how they feel that all learners' individual needs can best be met in one class?   Students might, for example, become responsible for working with the teacher and with other students to develop a plan for a project which both takes into account their strengths and helps them improve their weaknesses. The teacher can help learners understand that at times they will be working on different individual or group projects as the curriculum will become differentiated based on the unique learning needs of students.   In this way, students might become accustomed to working as a community of learners rather than as separate or competing entities and recognize that sometimes giving everyone the exact same quiz or assignment would be anything but fair.

Case 5

Mrs. Carney anxiously awaited the arrival of her kindergarten students. Although she had been teaching for twelve years, she was always apprehensive on the first day. She looked forward to preparing these children in a developmentally appropriate manner which, she felt, made the children more independent and self-directed. This had not always been her chosen philosophy, but while earning her master's degree she had found that developmentally appropriate practices were definitely better for the young child.

Shortly after class had begun, the door quietly opened and Kenya Jones along with her mother, Aleta Jones, walked in. Kenya was a very pretty, tall, blond girl. She was dressed very girlishly, yet overdressed for the warm climate. Mrs. Jones hung up Kenya's sweater, took the supplies from her backpack, and lead her to her seat. After several minutes, Mrs. Carney had to ask Mrs. Jones to leave. This occurred the next day as well.

On the third day of school, Mrs. Carney had an emergency and had a substitute in her classroom. When Mrs. Jones and Kenya arrived, late again, Mrs. Jones did not want to leave; the substitute had to send for the guidance counselor, Mrs. Fern, to persuade her to leave Kenya. This was the onset of Mrs. Carney's dilemma.

When Mrs. Carney returned to school and was informed of the incident, she decided to check Kenya's records. She found that Kenya was the right age to enter kindergarten; she had turned five in the previous spring. There was no home phone number on the enrollment form. The only way to contact the family was through the father at work. Mrs. Carney had also noticed that Mrs. Jones and Kenya walked to school.

Over the next several weeks, Kenya was often absent. Usually, no note was sent to explain her absences. When she did come to school, she would cry until her mother left. Mrs. Carney noticed that Kenya only observed in class, and did not interact with other students. She did not even perform parallel play. The other children had to lead Kenya around, often holding her hand. She had no eye contact with others, and she seldom smiled. Neither did Kenya stand straight; she had poor posture and seemed to shuffle as she walked. All of this indicated to Mrs. Carney that Kenya had poor self-esteem. While Kenya lacked gross motor skills, she had excellent fine motor control; her coloring and journal writing were always done well.

Due to Kenya's continued absences, Mrs. Carney sent Mrs. Jones a letter requesting that she come to the school for a conference. During the conference, Mrs. Carney asked Mrs. Jones if she would like to volunteer at school. However, because of the separation anxiety exhibited by Kenya, it would be better if Mrs. Jones worked in one of the other classrooms. This way, she would be close to Kenya throughout the day. Mrs. Carney also brought out the fact that Kenya did good work, but did not listen to directions. Instead, she copied what the other children were doing. In response, Mrs. Jones pulled out a five-page note that enumerated her objections to Mrs. Carney's teaching style.

Mrs. Jones asked, "what do the happy and sad faces reflect on the children's papers? Are they your personal feelings about the individual child?"

Mrs. Carney replied, "No, a happy face means they did a good job on their papers. A sad face means they could have done better."

Then Mrs. Jones said, "I don't like the open ramps; I think they are dangerous. Someone could just steal the children. Are the children allowed to leave the room by themselves?"

Responding to this question, Mrs. Carney stated, "No, they leave the room in small groups." At this point the red flag went up, and Mrs. Carney realized she was being placed in an awkward situation. She felt that the best thing to do was to continue the conference the next day with Mrs. Fern present.

The next afternoon Mrs. Jones' first comment was, "I do not want other children holding Kenya's hand."

Mrs. Carney replied, "If Kenya doesn't want other children holding her hand, then she needs to tell them. That's her responsibility. I am not her mother; I am her teacher."

Mrs. Jones questioned, "How can I make my child more assertive?"

At this time, Mrs. Fern interjected, "Kenya will not become assertive until you let her be more independent, and you become more assertive."

Mrs. Jones stated at this time, "I do not want Kenya to leave the room without you or another adult with her."

"If that is your request, then it must be in writing because it is not school policy," Mrs. Carney replied.

After the conclusion of this conference Mrs. Jones called the superintendent's office concerning Mrs. Fern's comment. She felt that the counselor was interfering with her family's personal life.

The superintendent's office contacted Mrs. Fern and told her she had no right to interfere with family home life.

From this point on, the situation with Mrs. Jones went downhill. The notes came daily, including the written request by Mr. And Mrs. Jones that Kenya was to be accompanied by an adult when she left the classroom. Mrs. Carney attempted to answer her notes, but she realized the effort was futile.

Kenya began wetting her pants at school. Since she could not be sent to the office alone, Mrs. Carney had to send another child for assistance. After several such incidents, the secretary contacted the father at work; he had to go get the mother, and together they came to pick up Kenya. Clothes were sent to school the next day accompanied by a note in which Mrs. Carney was blamed for not telling Kenya to go to the bathroom. Kenya never wet her pants at school again, so the problem was resolved.

After Christmas vacation, Mrs. Carney's class was to begin weekly small group trips to the library. Remembering the previous request, Mrs. Carney explained the procedure for the visits to Mrs. Jones. The parents decided that Kenya would be allowed to go as long as she went and returned with the group. On her group's second trip, the other children became tired of waiting for Kenya, and they returned to the room without her. Immediately realizing what had happened, Mrs. Carney rushed to open the door. At the same time, the librarian opened her door and they watched Kenya walk down the ramp to the classroom.

The next morning Mrs. Jones informed Mrs. Carney, "You have disobeyed my rules. What are you going to do about it?"

Mrs. Carney saw red! Instead of responding, she decided to confer with Mr. Relleum, the principal. Their decision was to switch the responsibility of Kenya's library privilege back to the parents.

That afternoon Mrs. Carney told Mrs. Jones, "If you want Kenya to use the library, you will have to take her after school because I cannot comply with your request."

For a while things seemed to go better. Kenya was adjusting socially to the class. Then, Kenya was absent for ten days, and when she returned, the old problems returned.

At the beginning of the second semester, Mrs. Jones was continuing to bring Kenya to school late, come into the classroom with her, unbutton her coat, hang it up, and set up her desk for the day.

Mrs. Carney reminded Mrs. Jones that school began at 7:30 a.m. and Kenya needed to be in her seat by that time, not at 7:45. Good-byes would be said outside the door.

Mrs. Jones then began her surveillance of the P.E. field. She complained about the number of children on the field at one time. However, when asked if she would like to volunteer to help, she refused, but her surveillance continued.

At Open House, when the father was asked by Mrs. Carney how he liked Kenya's school, he replied, "I don't see anything good here at all."

There were constant confrontations between parents and teacher. They usually began, "You must do something about ... " or "What did you do about ...?" This excessive documentation had begun to set up a vicious cycle. Mrs. Carney sought the help of Mr. Relleum; his response was "accommodate." The problem was put back into the classroom.

Kenya's excessive absence became another critical issue. Mrs. Carney would send missed class work home with Kenya, but it was never returned. Although the requests continued, Mrs. Carney tired of the useless chore. Once again she spoke with Mr. Relleum. Once again he told her to "accommodate -- in her own way."

The student had missed 60 days of school at this point. Since this was in excess of the allowed number of days, a letter was mailed to the parents informing them that Kenya was in danger of failing. There was no change in attendance. Mrs. Carney felt that Kenya was doomed for failure due to her established attendance pattern and lack of social skills. However, Kenya was academically promoted to the first grade.

The teachers reviewed their parent evaluations during post-planning. Mrs. Carney was appalled to discover that Mrs. Jones had rated her as an uncaring, unprofessional teacher. The bigger shock came two days later when she ran into Kenya and Mrs. Jones. Kenya ran up to her and hugged her; she excitedly told Mrs. Carney about the plans she and her mother had for the summer. Mrs. Carney haltingly replied, "That's nice."

What is pre-service candidates' analysis of the case? How does their analysis compare with that of the school faculty analysis which follows?

School Faculty Analysis: Case 5

Carol Bregman, Rebecca Francis, Cynthia Lasky, Mariolga Lebredo, Bertha Moro, Judy Newman, Doris Olesky, Mickey Weiner

Case Analysis

Step 1: Elements of the Problem

The school faculty concludes that the elements in this case include: (a) a distrustful, overprotective parent who is interfering with a teacher's attempt to assist a child in developing appropriate academic and social skill (b) a parent's and school's expectations are not in alignment and (c) there is a negative cycle of communication between parent, teacher and principal.

Step 2: Identifying the Facts

The group identified the following facts in the case:

1. Kenya is a student in Mrs. Carney's class.
2. Kenya was frequently tardy and absent from school.
3. When Kenya did come to school, she would cry until her mother left.
4. Mrs. Carney had to ask Mrs. Jones to leave the kindergarten class on several occasions so that her instructional program would not be interrupted.
5. Kenya did not interact with the other students.
6. Mrs. Carney conferred with Kenya's mother regarding Kenya's social and academic skills and also communicated with the school counselor and the principal to try to improve the situation.
7. Mrs. Jones was displeased with Mrs. Carney's teaching style, as well as the advice offered by the counselor.
8. After Mrs. Jones contacted the superintendent, the principal told Mrs. Carney that she must accommodate Kenya's parents.
9. Although Kenya missed more than 60 days of school, she was promoted to first grade at the end of the year.
10. Mrs. Jones rated Mrs. Carney as an uncaring, unprofessional teacher.

Step 3: Understanding the Problem

The group notes the following as having a bearing on the case:

1. Has Kenya had a physical or hearing test? Not listening and excessive absences may be associated with a medical condition.
2. Is the Jones family new to the district, state, country? This might help explain some of the miscommunication.
3. Did Kenya attend pre-K, nursery school or day care? If not, perhaps this explains why Mrs. Jones is so overprotective and is afraid to leave Kenya in the school's custody.
4. Has Kenya or her family experienced recent major changes or trauma? This might relate to the excessive absences and/or fear and mistrust.
5. Why is Kenya absent? Is she ill or is a family member ill, and her family therefore chooses to keep her home?
6. Has the family been connected to counseling services? This could help identify why there are so many struggles with communication, attendance, possible health issues or financial hardship.
7. What caused Kenya's poor self-esteem? Perhaps Kenya was criticized a lot at home, or there was some sort of verbal, physical or sexual abuse going on in the home. Perhaps being continuously tardy or absent from school made Kenya feel as though she was behind the other children.
8. Why did Mrs. Jones feel that Mrs. Fern was interfering in her family's personal life? Mrs. Jones might be hiding a family secret, or simply did not like people giving her advice on how to raise her child.
9. Why was Kenya wetting her pants? Did she wet her pants at home? This might have been an attention seeking behavior, or it may indicate a medical condition or even physical or sexual abuse.
10. Why didn't the principal support Mrs. Carney? He may be afraid of the parents (that they may complain to the district or school board). Did he have a personal problem with Mrs. Carney?
11. Why was Mrs. Jones so critical of the school? Was she always critical? Perhaps she simply wanted to intimidate Mrs. Carney or she has not felt comfortable with the school or its policies.

12. Why did Kenya never return missed homework sent home? Did Kenya show the homework to her parents. The parents may not feel it was their responsibility to help her with the homework, or that it was important to make-up missed work. Perhaps there was a language barrier and Kenya's parents could not help her.
13. Why was Kenya promoted even though she had missed more than the allowed number of missed days? Was the exception made to quiet complaining parents? Would Kenya benefit from repeating kindergarten? Who made this decision and upon what was it based?

Step 3: Relevant Knowledge Base

The group notes that answers to the following are predicated upon one having a sound knowledge of the following topics and ideas:

- Teacher/family expectations regarding the purpose of schooling.
- Physical examination/health screening for P-12 students.
- Family background and its effect on student performance.
- The background experience of the child and its impact on learning.
- Early childhood education and childhood development.
- School/family relations and communication.
- Attendance policies of the school or district.
- Retention/promotion policies of the school or district.

Step 4: Finding Assumptions

The school faculty sees the following taken for granted in the case, and notes the validity or invalidity of each:

- Parents and the school have similar expectations/goals for student. The group finds this assumption to be invalid based on professional service and expertise.
- Supportive schools and families benefit learners. The group finds this assumption to be valid when open communication exists between the home and the school and invalid when what is interpreted to be support by one is interpreted to be interference by another.

- Students can be affected academically and emotionally by conflicts between the home and school, though the student may not be able to express this discomfort. The group finds this assumption to be valid based on professional as well as personal experience.
- Attendance patterns can impact student achievement and development. The group finds this assumption to be valid.

Step 5: Detecting Arguments

The school faculty identified the following arguments in the case and noted errors in reasoning when appropriate:

- Parents want their children to succeed in school. Kenya is a child; therefore, her parents want her to succeed. The group perceives a four-term fallacy in this argument.
- Open communication between families and school can benefit students. Kenya is a student; therefore, open communication between the school and her family would benefit her. The group sees another four-term fallacy here as well.
- Preparing children in a developmentally appropriate manner makes them more independent and self-directed. Mrs. Carney teaches using developmentally appropriate practices; therefore, her students will be more independent and self-directed. If this argument is seen as a hypothetical syllogism, then the group sees the structure of the argument as valid (affirming the antecedent).
- Kenya is five years old. Five years old is the right age to enter kindergarten; therefore, Kenya is ready to enter kindergarten. According to the school faculty, as a categorical syllogism, the structure of the argument is valid.
- Students who don't interact with other children, don't parallel play, don't have eye contact and seldom smile lack social skills. Kenya displays these behaviors; therefore, Kenya lacks social skills. The group sees the structure of this argument as valid.
- Parents who are overprotective and critical of teachers, in general prevent their children from becoming independent and assertive. Mrs. Jones is an overprotective, critical parent; therefore, Kenya lacks independence and assertiveness. This argument does not follow according to the school faculty.

- When students are in regular attendance at school they develop socially and academically. Kenya was often absent from school; therefore, she was not developing socially or academically. The school faculty contends that the second premise in this argument denies the antecedent and therefore makes the conclusion invalid.

- When a student is absent excessively (more than the allowed number of days) he/she should not be promoted. Kenya was excessively absent; therefore, Kenya should not be promoted. According to the group, the hypothetical syllogistic structure of the argument is valid, but the initial premise does not follow.

Step 6: Interpretation of Case

In this case, one finds a continuous stream of confrontations occurring between the family of a kindergarten student and her teacher. The beliefs shared by the student's family seem repeatedly to be in direct contrast with the philosophy of the teacher as well as the aims and goals of the counselor and the school. Eventually, the disgruntled parent contacts the superintendent and the principal of the school tells the teacher that she must accommodate the parent.

At first glance, this case seems to illustrate how a lack of communication between the home and school can frustrate family members and teachers. However, if one recognizes that on dozens of occasions in this case the parents and school have been involved in either written, verbal or face to face communication, then there appears to be more of a communication gap than a lack thereof.

What began on the first day of school as a difference of opinion between teacher and parent (what kindergarten should look like) continued to escalate until the school year came to a close and the parents could not find anything positive in the school environment. How does one account for the chasm between parents and school becoming deeper with time?

There were differences of opinion between the school and home as to what sorts of behaviors and expectations should be fostered in a kindergarten class. But what was less obvious were attempts to understand both the ideas of the parents and the professional judgments of the teacher, for example. In other words, it appeared that the tone of the contacts between the family and the school never got beyond being confrontational or even hostile.

How might the year have gone had the school and the family tried to come to know each other's point of view? It did not appear that elements of trust were present at the conferences as the overall tone of the communication was judgmental and accusatory.

At one point during a conference, the parent asked the school counselor how she could help her child become more assertive. The counselor answered in such a way that the parent felt offended. One wonders again what may have happened if the tone of the conference would have been open and peaceful enough to invite the parent to a workshop, for example, given by the school and other parents who also had the same question as to how to develop independence in their children.

Perhaps a discussion as to how long the family has lived in its present location or the availability of a Parent Outreach Program which offers support for families with children in kindergarten would have offered the parent an opportunity to become connected with the school or other parents of children in the school so that the home/school relationship could be strengthened.

There were communication problems occurring within the school, as well. Each time a child is absent, a note must be received from the family, a doctor or clinic in order for the absence to be excused. When notes are not received, the policy of the school most likely refers repeated unexcused absences to a truancy program, such as the Truancy Intervention Program (TIP). Parents or legal guardians are responsible for their child's attendance, and the school is responsible for the proper implementation of its attendance policy. If this policy was familiar to Kenya's family and it was not enforced, it is no wonder that a lack of trust may have developed. Moreover, after missing more than 60 days of school, Kenya was promoted to first grade even after the teacher had sent a note home explaining that the child's absences were beyond the number allowable for promotion.

Here one finds another instance of a lack of clarity in communication between a school about it's retention policy and its behavior in promoting a child to the next grade.

Nevertheless, what one may find most unsettling about this case is that even with the dozens of contacts between the school and the family, questions regarding Kenya, her medical history, behavior at home, early childhood experiences, favorite things to do on weekends, and so on, never became part of the conversation. One still is unclear as to why she missed more than one third of the school year.

It is almost as if the year went by and no one really knows who Kenya is, the reasons for her missing so much school or coming late, or having difficulty interacting with others. Although one does learn about the good work she does in class, her neat journal or the difficulty she has following directions, only a sketch rather than a complete picture of Kenya seems to have been drawn.

Solution(s)

- Mrs. Carney might attempt to request a conference with Kenya's parents, the counselor, social worker, and other resource person to discuss her concerns with Kenya and go over her medical and social records, as well as establish goals and clarify school policies.

- Mrs. Carney might request that a school psychologist observe and evaluate Kenya and provide recommendations to family, counselor and principal.

- A visiting teacher or social worker might visit this home to gain an understanding of the home environment and how it may be affecting Kenya and her family. An understanding of Kenya's attendance patterns may be gleaned so that if the school can help her or her family in any way, the resources are made available.

- Mrs. Carney can request that the counselor invite an art therapist to observe and evaluate Kenya's art work.   Often children's emotional state and feelings are expressed in their art work.

- Mrs. Carney or the Parent Teacher Student Association might try encouraging Kenya's mother to become involved in the school's parent organization so she can have opportunities to get to know other parents, learn from them, and share her ideas with them.

- Since it was brought to the counselor's attention that Mrs. Jones wanted her daughter to become more assertive, the topic for the next parent in-service could incorporate suggestions for raising children to become independent. In this way, Kenya's mom would feel as though her concern is worthy of the school's attention, and she may begin to see the school as a worthwhile partner in her daughter's education.

- Home schooling may be a solution to this problem, if the parent chooses not to abide by school policies or if the family and school cannot come together and at least respect each other's point of view.

Case 6

Katherine is a young teacher at St. Mary's Catholic girls' school in the inner city of New York. Because St. Mary's is a private school, there are required tuition costs to attend. However, the school is the most heavily subsidized parish in New York City, and thus caters primarily to low income families. The students come from one of the worst areas in the city where poverty, crime, and drugs are a fact of life. The students say that if they want to get crack, it's not a matter of finding it, it's a matter of finding out which dealer has the best buy in the building. Parental support for students at the school is low, and as a result, the teachers are often the only positive role models available to the students.

This is Katherine's first teaching position, and her schedule includes teaching two health classes: one to freshmen and sophomores, and the other to juniors and seniors. Although her other classes are tracked, the health classes are not, and thus each is a mixture of varying learning abilities. Also, the textbooks offered are dated and do not include information on current problems, such as AIDS, that are important to her students. Although the administrators are aware of the problem, there are other subjects that demand priority.

One of the topics for discussion in Katherine's health class is sex, a controversial subject, particularly in the Catholic church. This school is part of the diocese under Bishop Kevin O'Conner who has been known to excommunicate parishioners who do not follow the Church's stance on issues concerning sex. The administrators at the school level are more tolerant as far as allowing unwed and expecting mothers to attend the school. However, they are still bound by the dictates of the Church concerning sex.

In a class of thirty-five girls, Katherine knows of eight who already have children of their own. Obviously, these students are sexually active, and she estimates that approximately 65% to 75% of the entire student body at St. Mary's is sexually active. Realizing that her duty as a good Catholic and as a teacher at a Catholic school is to expound the official beliefs of the Catholic Church, Katherine is torn between following the religious beliefs of her Church (with which she does not agree totally), or teaching these young girls (who are already known to be sexually active), about contraceptives. If she does so, she could be fired from her job and excommunicated.

If she does not, then there is a possibility that the girls will continue to have sex without knowledge of protection and be exposed to AIDS, more unwanted pregnancies, and even the termination of their education and thus the perpetuation of the *status quo*.

Is it possible for her to state, "This is the official stance of the Church and this school, but because you may not be adhering to this stance, here is some information that may protect you." Katherine is faced with a tough decision that involves her resolving her personal belief that the Holy Catholic Church is the ultimate authority representing her god, and her opinions as a young, modern, American woman and teacher, who is concerned about the welfare of her students.

Until this conflict is resolved, the fate of the young girls will hang in the balance.

What is pre-service candidates' analysis of the case? How does their analysis compare with that of the school faculty analysis which follows?

School Faculty Analysis: Case 6

Carol Bregman, Rebecca Francis, Cynthia Lasky, Mariolga Lebredo, Bertha Moro, Judy Newman, Doris Olesky, Mickey Weiner

Case Analysis

Step 1: Elements of the Problem

The school faculty concludes that the elements in this case include: (a) inadequate distribution of resources for current and up to date health information and (b) knowing where one's roles and responsibilities lie as a person, employee and/or a member of a social or religious group.

Step 2: Identifying the Facts in the Case

The group sees the following facts in the case:

1. Katherine is a young, first-year teacher at an inner-city Catholic school for girls.
2. The school is private, charges tuition and caters to low-income families.
3. Poverty, crime and use of drugs abound in the school's neighborhood.
4. Parental support in the school is low.
5. Katherine teaches health and the textbooks she has are out-of-date.
6. School administrators are aware that the health textbooks are inadequate.
7. Sex is a topic in Katherine's health class.
8. Administrators allow unwed and expecting mothers to attend the school.
9. Katherine is aware that eight of her students already have children and that others are sexually active.

10. Katherine is experiencing an inner-conflict between following strict church dictates and teaching about contraceptives and other topics that she feels will help her students.

Step 3: Understanding the Problem

The group identifies the following as having a bearing on the case even though not stated explicitly in the case:

1. Do Katherine's students feel they have a choice in their behavior? If students become aware that they have choices in their behaviors, they can perhaps become empowered to know themselves and the choices that may be best for them.
2. Is there any administrator or authority that can give current information on AIDS, contraception and other current health related topics? If the textbooks are outdated and money is not available, perhaps a guest speaker can be brought in as a human resource to share current information with Katherine's class.
3. Why are parents not involved in their children's education? If they are working perhaps it seems as though they are not involved even though they are trying their best.
4. What sort of parent outreach programs are available? Parent education can be a vital catalyst for family involvement.
5. What are the goals of Katherine's students? When students are able to focus on the future, they may make decisions that look more at tomorrow and less on day to day survival.
6. Has Katherine asked her administrators what the priorities should be for the students in her class? If an administrator takes a close look at what is happening, it is more likely that a compromise between religious ideals and personal beliefs might be made.
7. Has Katherine inquired as to what others in St. Mary's feel she should do to help her students? Perhaps, if Katherine finds an empathetic administrator, counselor or staff member, she might get some resources to update her textbooks or at least include up-to-date information on health education issues.

Step 3: Relevant Knowledge Base

The group notes that answers to the foregoing issues is predicated upon one having a sound knowledge (theoretical, empirical, craft wisdom, content) of the following concepts/ideas:

- Learning responsibility.
- Health information on AIDS and sexually transmitted diseases.
- Teenage pregnancy and its impact on students.
- School-parent communication.
- School governance.
- Decision-making.
- Religion and schools.
- Professional responsibility.
- Moral dilemmas.

Step 4: Finding Assumptions

The school faculty sees the following things taken for granted in the case:

- High school students can benefit by receiving health education. The group finds this assumption to be valid.
- Since health is not one of the most important subjects in the high school curriculum, current health textbooks are not essential. The group finds this assumption to be invalid in the sense that current information is useful yet the group also realizes that information in textbooks may be already out of date by the time books are published. In addition, courses may be taught without textbooks.
- Unwed and expecting mothers can benefit by attending school. The group finds this assumption to be valid in some cases and not valid in others.
- Knowledge of sex education and contraceptives can benefit students. The group finds this assumption to be valid based on professional experience.
- Church doctrine and personal choice may be in conflict. The group finds this assumption to be valid in some cases and invalid in others.

Step 5: Detecting Arguments

The group identified the following arguments in the case:

- The Catholic church says no to contraception. Katherine teaches in a Catholic school; therefore, Katherine must not teach about contraception. The school faculty notes a four-term fallacy in this argument's structure.
- AIDS and contraception are topics in health education. Katherine is a health educator; therefore, she can teach about AIDS and contraception. The group believes this argument to contain a *non-sequitur*.
- The environment surrounding St. Mary's school is filled with drugs, crime and poverty. Students may be influenced by their environment; therefore, Katherine's students are influenced by drugs, crime and poverty. Again, the group finds this argument to contain a four-term fallacy.
- Some students in St. Mary's are unwed and expecting mothers. Students who attend school can benefit by becoming educated, therefore unwed and expecting mothers in St. Mary's school should attend school. The group notes that this argument commits the fallacy of undistributed middle.
- If one is religious then one must obey the rules of the church. Katherine is religious; therefore, she must obey the rules of the church. While the group finds the structure of the hypothetical syllogism to be valid, it is concerned with the weak relationship between the antecedent and consequent in the first premise.
- All persons can think and act independently. Katherine is a person; therefore, she can think and act independently. The group finds the categorical syllogistic structure of this argument to be valid.

Step 6: Interpretation of Case

Katherine is a high school health teacher in an inner-city Catholic school who is aware that many of her students are sexually active. Although her own personal beliefs seem to favor a more open approach with her students regarding the teaching of issues related to human sexuality, sexually transmitted diseases, AIDS and contraception, her superior and the official church doctrine are severely opposed.

On the one hand, Katherine is afraid of losing her job if she does not adhere strictly to religious doctrines espoused by the Catholic Church. Yet on the other hand, she is aware that her students' welfare, future and possibly lives are in danger.

Katherine's is a moral dilemma. Is she bound by church policy to teach abstinence only in sex education, or is she to be true to her own instincts that urge her to teach young people methods of contraception that would protect them against sexually transmitted disease and AIDS? Should she help them to make choices? According to Kohlberg's stages in the development of moral values, Katherine seems to be struggling with morality of conventional role-conformity vs. self-accepted moral principles (1967). It appears that in order for Katherine to uphold her own personal morals and professional responsibilities, she must do whatever she can to provide for the safety and well-being of her students, even if there is a risk factor involved.

There is a contradiction in the policy that allows unwed and expectant mothers to attend the school in direct opposition to the Bishop of diocese, who has been known to impose severe sanctions on parishioners who deviate from the church's stand on issues concerning sex. At least some of the school administrators seem obviously to be more tolerant and lenient in their interpretation of church doctrine. The teacher, then, might see this as her opportunity to bend the dictate to permit her to include information in her teaching that would protect and forewarn young people who are openly engaging in sexual relations.

Solution(s)

- Since Katherine is aware of some of the challenges her students face, she might hold ongoing classroom discussions or rap sessions focused on topics connected to the real world of her students, such as: stresses facing teenagers, making safe and informed decisions, the courage to choose what is best, behaviors and their consequences, planning for the future, how to choose a friend, and toward an understanding of myself. On some days, Katherine might select the topic, and on other days, her students could select the topic of their choice. As a follow-up activity, students could complete an entry in their journals which further explores the topic and the students' thoughts and feelings.

- Katherine might find the ear of a lenient administrator, possibly to get official approval of her handling sensitive issues in the health curriculum and in her classroom.
- Health educators, nurses and doctors could be invited frequently to the classroom to dispense current and up-to-date health information which the outdated texts may not contain.
- Katherine might wish to collaborate with other faculty members. Perhaps the school could start a parent outreach program to try to improve family involvement.

Case 7

The year is 1999, and Wiley Thomas, the principal at P.S. #62 in Tipton, Connecticut, is confronted by two of his middle school teachers, Mr. Burdine and Mrs. Mitkevicius regarding Bobby Brown, an eleven year old sixth grader. Each teacher has a different view of Bobby, and of how he can best be taught.

Mr. Burdine is Bobby's homeroom teacher and a former elementary school principal in Tipton. He had been a principal from 1996-1999, and a former associate of Mr. Thomas. Prior to that time, he taught in the elementary school system for five years. In 1999, the school board chose not to renew Mr. Burdine's contract as a principal. He was hired by Mr. Thomas prior to the beginning of the current semester.

Mr. Burdine is an authoritarian. His classroom and students reflect his managerial style. The classroom is immaculate, well organized, and structured to accommodate his lectures. His students are orderly and well-mannered. To Mr. Burdine, there is a time and place for everything and everybody.

Mrs. Mitkevicius is only in her second year of teaching. She is still developing her classroom managerial style, but it is evident that on whatever style she will settle, it will contrast markedly with that of Mr. Burdine's. Her classroom appears to be in complete disarray most of the time. Her classes are much like Grand Central Station at rush hour with children moving here and there, doing this and that, while she oversees their activity. To her credit, she knows where everything and everyone is at all times. Her students think she is "cool," and she is well liked by the teaching staff. Like Mr. Burdine, she too was hired by Mr. Thomas.

It is Mr. Burdine's contention that Bobby should be placed in a special school where the teachers are better equipped to handle and train him. He feels that Bobby will receive far superior training and be catered to at a special school, and the individualized instruction that he will receive will be better for him in the long run. More importantly, Bobby will not be a disruptive force in and around others like himself. According to Mr. Burdine, it is impossible to teach with an eleven year old crawling around the classroom floor acting like a dog or cat. Bobby has a propensity for doing this, and Mr. Burdine finds this to be very upsetting to him and his class.

Bobby's grades are another item of contention in this case. Bobby is not a gifted child. His academic record shows that he reads at a second grade level, and that he is academically well below others in his class. Based on Bobby's disruptive behavior, and his grades, Mr. Burdine is strongly recommending that Mr. Thomas place Bobby in a special school where his educational needs can be met properly, and his behavioral needs addressed.

Mrs. Mitkevicius, on the other hand, is strongly opposed to such action. She feels such measures are too drastic, and are uncalled for in Bobby's case. To her, Bobby is no different than any of her other students. She agrees that he has emotional and academic problems, but she argues that he is capable of functioning in the standard classroom. Even when Bobby is doing his thing, Mrs. Mitkevicius feels there is no problem in the classroom. She has explained to her class that all human beings are different, and that they must recognize and deal with these differences throughout their lives. She encourages her students to accept Bobby for what he is, not what they want him to be. To her, Bobby's behavior is his norm, and it simply needs to be understood by those around him. She argues that Bobby's actions should not be disturbing, if one takes the time to understand Bobby.

Mrs. Mitkevicius also feels that Bobby is quite capable of learning and being taught. She points out that there are "normal" students who are poor readers and well below their classmates academically, and they are not alienated. So, why Bobby? Mrs. Mitkevicius tells Mr. Thomas that it will be wrong to put Bobby in a special class or school because of his behavior, which although different, can be worked around. She adds that her class is proof of this.

The last point Mrs. Mitkevicius raises is in the form of a question. She asks, "Is Bobby's transfer out of regular classes really going to be beneficial to him?" Without awaiting an answer she adds, "I don't believe so." She says that it is in Bobby's best interest that he remain with his class. Here, he can socialize and learn with normal students, and this will be better for him than having him placed into a class or school where abnormal behavior is the norm.

Mr. Thomas having listened to both teachers' arguments realizes the magnitude of this decision and knows that he will be branded no matter what decision he makes. What would you do if you were Mr. Thomas?

What is pre-service candidates' analysis of the case? How does their analysis compare with that of the school faculty analysis which follows?

School Faculty Analysis: Case 7

Carol Bregman, Rebecca Francis, Cynthia Lasky, Mariolga Lebredo,
Bertha Moro, Judy Newman, Doris Olesky, Mickey Weiner

Case Analysis

Step 1: Elements of the Problem

The school faculty concludes from its dialogue that the elements in
this case are as follows: (a) what is the best learning environment for
Bobby? (b) is there one best match between one's teaching style and a
student's learning style? and (c) should the educational philosophy of a
teacher affect a student's classroom placement?

Step 2: Identifying the Facts in the Case

The group sees the following facts in the case:

1. Bobby is an 11 year old sixth grader who is reading on a second
   grade level.
2. Bobby has a propensity for crawling on the floor like a dog/cat.
3. Mr. Burdine is Bobby's homeroom teacher; he is authoritarian.
4. Mrs. Mitkevicius is also Bobby's teacher; her style is more
   casual.
5. Mrs. Burdine feels that Bobby should be placed in a special
   school, while Mrs. Metkevicius feels that Bobby's needs can be
   better met if he remains in a standard educational program.

Step 3: Understanding the Problem

The group identifies the following as having a bearing on the case
even though they are not explicitly in the case:

1. Have the teachers checked Bobby's records for previous
   behavior problems? Student records would show if he has a
   history of disruptive behavior and how it was handled.

2. Have previous teachers been contacted about Bobby's problems? How did they deal with Bobby? Perhaps they used strategies that could be used now to help this student.

3. How is Bobby's behavior in Mr. Burdine's room? In Mrs. Mitkevicius' room? Are the same behaviors or behavioral patterns observable?

4. What sort of progress is Bobby making in each of his classrooms? Is progress measured by the same means?

5. What subjects do Mr. Burdine and Mrs. Mitkevicius teach? If one teacher is an academic subject teacher and the other is, for example, a special area teacher such as art, music or physical education, different sets of expectations and/or pressures may exist for Bobby and for the teacher. Different classroom environments and different teaching styles may impact Bobby's behavior.

6. Is Bobby prescribed any medication to control his abnormal behavior? If so, perhaps the dosage is incorrect and he is suffering side effects. An evaluation by a physician may be in order as health issues can contribute to academic and emotional behavior.

7. Have the parents been contacted about Bobby's behavior and academic standing? A conference could enlighten the situation as to home environment, siblings, and changes in the family structure, all of which may affect a student's attitude, behaviors and ability to learn.

8. Has Bobby received tutoring to help raise his academic level? Has it helped, or is Bobby doing the best he can? If Bobby is doing the best he can, the frustration at not doing better could be the basis of his behavior.

9. How do the other students feel about Bobby? If there is a sense of community in the classrooms, other students may benefit by reaching out and helping Bobby. If they feel he is interrupting the environment, they may alienate Bobby, which would impact Bobby's need for attention negatively.

10. Does the school have a child study team or plan in place for referring students who need help? These teams take teacher observations, psychological testing, academic level and other data in order to evaluate a student's needs for special services. Going through this process would help find Bobby's strengths and weaknesses.

Step 3: Relevant Knowledge Base

The group notes that answers to the foregoing issues is predicated upon one's having a sound knowledge (theoretical, empirical, craft wisdom, content) of the following concept/ideas, etc.:

- Educational governance of schools.
- Teacher expectations.
- Teaching and learning styles.
- Philosophy of education.
- Childhood development.
- Teacher rights.
- Labeling.
- Teacher and parent conferences.
- Assessing student learning.
- School policy regarding student referrals.

Step 4: Finding Assumptions

The school faculty sees the following taken for granted in the case, and identifies those assumptions that may be invalid based on evidence in the case or current professional knowledge:

- Mrs. Metkivicius' classroom is disorganized and learning cannot happen there. Based on school realities, it is not a valid assumption since professional would suggest that learning is not necessarily dictated by the organization or appearance of one's classroom.
- Special schools are better equipped to meet the needs of special students. Based on professional knowledge, this is a valid assumption when the teachers, students and program work to meet the needs of the child and an invalid assumption when they do not.
- Bobby's grades and behavior may result in his being labeled a special student and placed in a special school or program. Current school reality and policy combine to make this a valid assumption.

- It is impossible to teach with an eleven-year-old crawling on the floor like a dog/cat. Based on some teachers' perceptions, this would be a valid assumption although it would be an invalid assumption to teachers who may accept the challenge to turn this situation into a possible teachable moment.
- Abnormal behavior is the norm in special schools. The group determines this assumption to be invalid based on personal and professional experience.
- Bobby learns in Mrs. Metkivicius' room. The new teacher in this case holds to this assumption which according to school reality could be a valid assumption.
- Students with abnormal behavior do not belong with other students. According to professional knowledge, this is a valid assumption in some cases, invalid in others.

Step 5: Detecting Arguments:

The group identified the following arguments in the case; arguments held by characters in the case or imbedded in some decision:

- Special schools have teachers better able to handle and train children with problems. P.S.#62 is not a special school; therefore, the teachers at P.S. #62 cannot handle children with problems. The school faculty feels that this argument begs the question.
- Special schools meet the educational and behavioral needs of special students. Bobby's has special needs; therefore, Bobby's needs can be met in a special school. The group feels that the conclusion does not necessarily follow from the premises.
- Students who are poor readers and low academically are alienated. Bobby is a poor reader with low grades; therefore, Bobby is alienated. The group finds the argument to be irrelevant.
- Bobby can socialize and learn with normal students. Special schools have students with abnormal behavior; therefore, Bobby should not be placed in a special school. This argument, the group feels, contains a four-term fallacy.

Step 6: Interpretation of Case

The case centers around a philosophical difference of opinion in the correct placement of a student with low academic ability and behavioral problems. An experienced teacher who runs a well-organized classroom feels the student belongs in a special school; another teacher whose environment is less structured feels the student should remain in a regular school setting. The bottom line of the problem is what is the best school environment for Bobby.

When one is faced with the question as to what is the best school environment for Bobby, one can first begin to determine what factors determine the best placement for any student, since one may assume that all learners deserve opportunities to develop and learn, despite their special needs.

In Bobby's case, however, he has been described by one teacher as having educational and behavioral needs which can best be met by being placed in a special school. A second teacher prefers to describe Bobby as having emotional and academic problems which are no different than her other students. One may wonder why there seems to be only a choice between these two teachers or between a standard placement in his current school and a special placement in a different school.

In addition, the case does not state if the child has been referred to be tested and evaluated by the school district's educational psychologist. Given the battery of paperwork which needs to be completed before a child is tested, and the fact that once the paperwork is completed, the child may or may not qualify for any sort of special education, the discussion as to whether or not to place Bobby in a special class or program seems to be a bit premature.

On the one hand, it is difficult to say where is the best place to put Bobby when one does not know the choices which exist. On the other hand, the best place to put Bobby or any child is in an educational environment in which the child will be honored as a human being, and allowed to succeed by contributing to the classroom in a variety of ways. A teacher who is able and willing to help a child with academic, social or emotional problems and strengthen a child's sense of self may benefit not only Bobby but any learner who is a member of a classroom family.

It is stated in the case that Bobby is "not gifted" because his academic skills are below grade level. However, Mrs. Mitkevicius seems to be willing to challenge the assumption that giftedness is solely an academic matter. She contends that he is able to learn and be taught. Perhaps the theory of multiple intelligence supported by Gardner (1993) would be useful to Mrs. Mitkevicius and Bobby since the concept of intelligence is more broadly defined than relying on strictly abilities related to language or mathematics. Does he have musical ability? Is he an artist or a scientist? Although the case does mention that he is academically well below other students, additional information cold be useful to know so that Bobby and his teachers could use his interests and talents to build up his weak areas.

Teacher expectations may also impact a student's behavior and academic performance. Mrs. Mitkevicius seems to focus on what Bobby can do rather than what he cannot. Her expectations that he will learn may be more likely to communicate to him that he is expected to try. There is some evidence in the case that Mr. Burdine may not expect much from Bobby, and a self-fulfilling prophecy may deliver to Mr. Burdine the empty package he expects to receive.

On the other hand, Mrs. Mitkevicius appears to have an open mind as far as what she expects Bobby to accomplish. Her attitude that he can learn in her classroom may be communicated to Bobby in many direct and indirect ways. Since she expects him to learn, she, too, may get what she expects.

If Bobby perceives that he is in a safe and flexible learning environment, he may not be afraid to take a risk at learning something new. Given the two different classroom environments and the two potentially contrasting sets of expectations which may exist for Bobby, it may seem as though Bobby is in a no-win situation if he remains in Mr. Burdine's classroom. However, before deciding which is the best learning environment for Bobby, one might consider other factors, as well. Which classroom does Bobby prefer? Why?

Suppose one assumes that since Mrs. Mitkevicius seems more compassionate toward Bobby, her classroom would automatically be the best place for him, yet Bobby explains that he cannot learn as well in her room or that he gets headaches from highly interactive environments, excessive noise or clutter? One is not sure from the case how Bobby's behavior varies in the two teachers' classrooms or which classes or subjects or time(s) of day Bobby's behavior improves or declines, or if his behavior is consistent regardless of the aforementioned factors. Therefore, although on the surface it may appear that the less authoritarian and more accepting environment of Mrs. Mitkevicius' classroom is the better place for Bobby, some additional action research may enhance the decision making process.

When contemplating the question of whether or not there is a best fit for teachers and learners based on a teacher's philosophy of education, perhaps a more critical response would be to redirect the question. Rather than looking for the perfect fit or the best match, a teacher can try to help learners become aware that different teaching and learning styles certainly exist. Perhaps learners can more aptly recognize that no matter who the teacher is or what style is present, something positive can be learned if one accepts the responsibility for one's own learning. It may be useful to help learners recognize and question a teacher's philosophy so that learners can begin to have an awareness of their own beliefs about schooling versus education, for example, or how and why certain students get placed into certain classrooms or programs.

Although there may be some educational philosophies or beliefs held by teachers that more comfortably incorporate a student's learning style or unique characteristics, teachers and students may benefit by being exposed to a variety of diverse styles. These exposures to diverse learning environments can actually help one reinforce or strengthen one's own educational philosophy. One would not want to assume that because a teacher's style or philosophy is more structured that only structured thinkers can learn in the classroom or that students can only learn when a teacher's style is in line with a learner's preference.

If Bobby's principal decides to change him to a different class, there would likely be many factors considered which directly relate to philosophy of education and beliefs about who can learn and in what ways. However, using a philosophy of education as the sole determinant as to where to place students seems a bit shortsighted. A principal should not only hire teachers whose philosophies match his or her own.

Solution(s)

- Every student has a file/cumulative folder that follows him/her through his/her school career. The file contains information concerning health issues, language needs, standardized test scores, progress reports and documentation of special needs.

Most teachers will go to this information bank when they perceive that one of their students is behaving out of the range of the average student. Bobby's 6th grade teachers may wish to check his cumulative folder and collaborate with any of his past teachers as to teaching and learning strategies which may have been particularly effective.

- Bobby's teachers may wish to request a conference with Bobby's parents. Further meetings with counselors and administrators may be useful to gain more insight into what is required to meet Bobby's special needs.

- If parents and school staff agree, Bobby can be referred for the evaluation process, which will use observations, health screenings, and psychological testing to diagnose his strengths and weaknesses. These findings will be used to write a personal education plan for this student, placing him in the least restrictive environment necessary for his special learning needs. This is a county mandated procedure. Using teacher observations and personal beliefs is only a part of the whole procedure.

- Perhaps placing some of the responsibility on Bobby to help teachers determine one or more behavioral or academic goals will help him realize that although the teachers are willing to work with him to help him improve, he must try to maintain some focus on his work and behavior and help himself. Perhaps he can keep a log of his behaviors and rate himself as to how hard he thinks he is trying in each class and why. A discussion with Bobby and his parents or teachers may include such topics as: Is Bobby happy with his behavior? Does Bobby want to improve? Does he feel he knows how to improve? In what ways can he improve? How can his family and teachers help him improve?

- Perhaps Bobby would be motivated by having a mentor or a learning buddy. Sometimes when a child's skill levels are weak, peer tutoring can help. Working cooperatively with another student or in small groups can also help Bobby learn and practice social skills at the same time academic and emotional needs may be addressed.

- Bobby and the other children could complete an interest inventory which indicates their favorite subjects, hobbies, stories, etc. These data could perhaps be used by Bobby's teachers to help him develop a project to share with classmates.

If there is another child who has a similar interest, perhaps this project can become a group project so that Bobby feels needed and supported by his learning partner.

Case 8

Mary West, the teacher for the Emotionally Handicapped at Woodrow High School, is faced with a difficult problem. It is three months into the school year and she has come to the conclusion that the in-school Guidance Committee, on which she serves, is not functioning properly and something must be done to correct it.

Mary is fully certified in Elementary Education and Emotionally Handicapped Education K-12. She had taught in a regular elementary classroom in Chicago for seven years before teaching Emotionally Handicapped. This is her first year at Woodrow High School. Prior to this position, Mary had worked teaching E.H. in Louisiana for five years. During this time, she served on a well functioning Guidance Committee, where the teaching staff, school administration, and even the parents carved out a clear idea of what constituted a good Guidance Committee.

Mary's evident assumption was that most schools had a well functioning Guidance Committee. Now she fears that the students' welfare is being neglected by the discord between the members of Woodrow's Guidance Committee and by the lack of interest on the part of the school administrators.

Since school started, the Guidance Committee has been meeting twice a month, and during this time, the teachers serving on this committee have been rotating chairpersonship each month - a policy established the previous year. Mary feels this is a very poor method, as forms and other information are being lost in the shift. Mary has also noticed that neither of the three counselors has attended the meetings, and the other members of the committee are doing 90% of the counselors' work. The teachers are angry because they feel they do most of the work and receive no recognition and/or extra pay. Any work which could only be done by the counselors had to be hand-delivered and one would have to wait while their part was done or return after a time to collect paperwork to make sure it was done. This added much extra work on the teachers who were trying to conduct the business of this committee and their own classroom work. They were not allowed extra time to accomplish these duties. Even, and more important, she was faced with the fact that the legalities were not being observed. Evaluations were not being completed in a timely fashion by the counselors unless one "stood over them."

There are laws stating how much time (and not more than) should elapse between when parents give consent to evaluate and when the evaluations are completed. These guidelines and others were not being met. Counselors had no reservations about post-dating forms. Of great concern to Mary was the fact that the state was to hold a county-wide audit on these records the following year. Money could be withdrawn from programs which were not conducting business correctly. Mary felt that this could happen to their program in these circumstances.

After much thought, Mary decided to volunteer to chair the committee for the remainder of the year. She arranged for a special meeting of the committee to be held a day before the regularly scheduled meeting and asked the three counselors to be present. She called for discussion of policy and the importance of establishing and enforcing a good working policy for the Guidance Committee. She concluded by stating that each member of the committee should be strongly positive in his/her attitude towards the committee if the result of their efforts was to be of benefit to the students of Woodrow High School.

Each member then voiced his/her opinions and grievances. All of the counselors said that they had no time to meet and/or chair the committee. They felt that they did not have time to obtain social history, contact parents, and conduct other Guidance Committee business in a timely manner. Their resentment was compounded by the fact that Mr. Hutchins, the school principal, had designated them as hall monitors among other duties.

Miss Avery, one of the counselors, said she would agree to have her name head the Guidance Committee, but wanted Mary to conduct the meetings.

Paul Overstreet, another counselor, was very belligerent and said he had had enough of Mary's and other teachers' constant "pushing." He said that "the Guidance Committee is not my boss" and that he had "enough to do with the smart ones who are clearly college-bound, and anyway, what difference do you think this committee makes with kids who can barely decipher words -- let the administration find a solution for absenteeism." And with this parting shot, he walked out of the meeting.

Mrs. Hale, the third counselor, was very upset and embarrassed about Mr. Overstreet's conduct and his attitude toward the less fortunate students.

She admitted the lack of participation on the part of the counselors, but informed the committee that she was also having trouble finding the time to attend the meetings, because in addition to her counseling, and hall monitoring duties, Mr. Hutchins had assigned her to teach a typing class a few periods a day.

While a lot of the committee members' feelings were brought to light, no solutions were found at the meeting. So Mary decided to speak to Mr. Hutchins to ask if he could help rectify the problem. He did not have or seem to want to have much knowledge of the situation. And his response was that the committee members should "handle the problem and quit making trouble."

Mary had to make a decision. She knew what must be done, but also knew that if she followed this course of action, her job would be in jeopardy, and at the very least, her relationship with Mr. Hutchins and some of the counselors would be extremely uncomfortable.

At the meeting the next day, Mary proposed that a meeting be held with the Director of Guidance and Teaching from the central office administration in charge of guidance committees for the county and with the Special Education head of attendance. She proposed to present the problem and ask for guidance in light of the upcoming audit, to have counselors released from all teaching duties, and to have all counselors released from hall monitor and other such duties.

What is pre-service candidates' analysis of the case? How does their analysis compare with that of the school faculty analysis which follows?

School Faculty Analysis: Case 8

Carol Bregman, Rebecca Francis, Cynthia Lasky, Mariolga Lebredo, Bertha Moro, Judy Newman, Doris Olesky, Mickey Weiner

Case Analysis

Step 1: Elements of the Problem
  The school faculty concludes that the following are elements in the case: (a) school climate (b) lack of communication and professional collaboration, and (c) ethics.

Step 2: Identifying the Facts

1. Mary perceives discord among teachers and counselors as well as a lack of interest by administrators.
2. Mary is trying to improve the guidance committee which meets twice each month.
3. Some counselors have not attended any guidance committee meetings. They feel overworked as they are assigned extra duties.
4. Some teachers are angry because they feel the counselors' jobs are not being performed properly which in turn makes extra work for teachers.
5. Faculty members are being asked to postdate forms in order to prepare for a county-wide state audit.
6. The school could lose funding based on the audit's findings which causes Mary to worry that the children's needs will continue to be inadequately met.

Step 3: Understanding the Problem

The group sees the following as having a bearing on the case:

1. Does the county have a prescribed format for this committee? Are minutes and agendas monitored? If this is the case, Mary can refer to the county policy for guidance in chairing this committee.

2. Is there a teachers' union? Do these counselors and teachers belong? The contract would have specific job descriptions. The principal would be aware of the contract. Are these extra duties allowed?

3. Are all of the counselors required to attend the guidance committee meetings? Their refusing to do so could perhaps result in an unsatisfactory evaluation.

4. Why is Mr. Hutchins so disinterested and uninformed about the committee? Bringing in the Director might spark his interest.

5. Is Mary the only teacher concerned with this situation? Are any other teachers, counselors or administrators concerned about the audit? Mary will need support in the meeting with the Director.

6. Will the audit cite the poorly functioning committee or are minutes being manufactured in some way? If the auditors monitor the documentation of meetings, they will perhaps notice the guidance committee's shortcomings.

7. Do any of the counselors have reservations about post-dating forms? Whose job status could be affected by the post-dated forms or other unethical forms of documentation?

8. Who will be present at the meeting with the Director? Mr. Hutchins, as building administrator must know the requirements of this committee. All participants, teachers, counselors and administrators must have the same information on the requirements of the guidance committee.

9. Is the school overpopulated? Understaffed? Under-resourced? This might explain why staff's job roles are shared or blurred.

10. Are there laws stating how much time can elapse between parental consent for evaluations and receiving services? If these guidelines are not being met, then laws or policies are being broken by the school.

Step 3: Relevant Knowledge Base

The group notes that answers to the foregoing issues is predicated upon one's having a sound knowledge of the following concept/ideas, etc.:

- School climate.
- Morale and attitudes.
- School leadership.

- Building a community of learners.
- Guidance and counseling.
- School priorities or mission.
- Problem solving.
- Collaboration.
  Funding of Exceptional Student Education Program (ESE) / state audit.
- Policy for evaluating children.
- School district Director of ESE.
- Job roles and descriptions for teachers and support staff personnel.
- Paid supplements.
- Teacher's union.
- Ethics.

Step 4: Finding Assumptions

The school faculty sees the following taken for granted in the case:

- Most schools have a well-functioning guidance committee. The group finds this assumption to be valid when the school's guidance committee is working effectively and invalid when schools either do not have a committee or have a dysfunctional committee.
- There is resentment between teachers and counselors. Based on professional experience, the group finds this assumption to be valid in cases such as Woodrow High and invalid when there is a sense of community amongst faculty members in a school.
- A positive attitude and school climate will impact the school and students in a positive way. The group finds this assumption to be generally true and valid.
- Students can benefit from a guidance team that functions smoothly; students can suffer when a well - functioning team is not in place. The professional knowledge of this group finds this assumption to be valid.
- A well-functioning guidance team is more likely to happen when all members communicate on a regular basis and assume responsibilities. The group finds this assumption to be valid based on professional experience.

- Situations can improve through communication and effort. Herein lies a valid assumption according to the professional knowledge of the group.
- College bound students deserve and/or require more attention from a counselor than do non-readers. Based on professional knowledge the group finds this assumption to be invalid.
- Faculty members in a school are expected at times to do things that are not specifically stated in one's contract or job responsibility. Based on the professional knowledge and experience of the group the assumption is valid.
- If administrators are unaware of a problem within the school, it either does not exist or it is not too serious. The group finds this assumption to be invalid based on professional knowledge.

Step 5: Detecting Arguments

The group identified the following arguments in the case:

- Schools should have a well-functioning guidance committee. Woodrow High is a school; therefore, the guidance committee should be well-functioning. The group finds this argument to be valid.
- Positive attitudes towards the guidance committee could result in a benefit to the students. Some students and counselors have a negative attitude towards the guidance committee; therefore, students will not benefit from the committee. This argument, according to the group, commits a four-term fallacy.
- If a principal is disinterested in an important component of the school, a person should seek outside help. Mr. Hutchins is disinterested in the guidance committee; therefore Mary should seek outside help. The group feels that there is no substantive connection between the antecedent and the consequent in the first premise of the argument.
- Money can be withdrawn from programs not correctly run. Woodrow High's guidance program is not being run correctly; therefore, money can be withdrawn from Woodrow's guidance program. The group finds that this argument does not follow.

Step 6: Interpreting the Case

A teacher of emotionally handicapped children feels the guidance committee on which she serves is not functioning properly and something must be done to correct it. The teacher fears students' welfare is being neglected by the staff's discord and administration's lack of interest.

It seems clear from the case that having a well-functioning guidance committee is not a high priority of the school administration. What is unclear, however, is why this would be so. One finds it difficult to understand how any high school (which has three counselors) would for some reason choose not to benefit from a well-defined guidance committee. Who among students, families, teachers and all faculty members would not benefit by the services and resources that a guidance committee could provide?

Nevertheless, Mary is a member of the guidance committee and she intends on improving it primarily so that the students can be well-served.

Although the guidance committee meets twice per month, the committee seems to be without a clear purpose. One wonders how effective the meetings can be when there are at times no counselors present. One also wonders how efficient the meetings can be when the chairperson rotates each month and there seems to be little continuity and a lot of confusion

In Woodrow High, the roles of faculty (teachers and counselors) seem to be separate and ill-defined, and therefore, frustration exists for those who know that collaboration and cooperation are "musts" for a school to adequately meet the needs of its students.

Mary has noted that there is a lack of interest and low morale within her faculty. But one wonders how morale could be anything but low when counselors are asked to teach typing, monitor hallways and falsify documents which is not only an unethical but an illegal activity. How could the school climate be anything but negative when teachers are expected to assume some of the counselors' workload in addition to classroom responsibilities? It appears that the number of contract violations which are transpiring may be too vast to count.

Solution(s)

- The guidance committee is in need of a clear plan and purpose that is supported by all of its members. Perhaps Mary can share a plan from one of her previous schools which worked well to use as a model and then the committee can create its own expectations and goals.
- Since Mary is new to the school, perhaps she can replicate some of the ideas that were effective in one of her other schools. She might try one idea at a time in order to try to establish a more positive school climate. For example, a faculty book club or after school yoga class may be a starter to bring people together on a personal level so that perhaps during the school day collaboration can occur on a professional level. Mary may wish to first meet with other faculty members to gain their support so that when they meet with the administration, she is not alone.
- If the guidance committee wishes to share responsibility for its leadership, perhaps a different member can co-chair with one consistent director or coordinator so that continuity is maintained each month.
- A member of the faculty can invite a guest speaker from the Office of Professional Standards to lead a presentation or dialog on issues of professionalism and ethical practices.
- A membership drive for the teachers' union can be held at which time matters related to job roles, responsibilities or other contractual concerns can be discussed.
- The building steward from the school or a representative from the teachers' union might approach the administration as to the availability of comp time or paid supplement positions so that when teachers or counselors take on additional job responsibilities, perhaps they will be compensated.
- Monthly breakfast bashes can be held for all faculty members at which time socializing and peer collaboration can occur.
- When Mary meets with the county Director, this person can suggest strategies and guidelines so that Woodrow High can meet the requirements of the ESE state audit and the guidance program can continue to function for the benefit of the students.
- Team building activities or a weekend retreat might be considered for this faculty to improve its morale and work together more cohesively as a community of learners.

When the school is seen as a community, teachers, counselors, parents, administrators, etc. can all come together and work as a team for the benefit of the learners.

- The school might invite a professor from a nearby university to discuss and administer the <u>Humanistic Climate Scale</u> (Dottin, 1984) as an effort to understand and improve the school climate.

Case 9

Mrs. Bartlett sighed thinking of what her next hour would probably be like. She had been dealing with behavior problems in her fifth-period English class for many weeks. The instigator, Jonathan Matthews, had not been responding very positively to her mild attempts at correction. In fact, correction seemed to negatively reinforce his behavior by giving him the attention he constantly craved. "Today I will see if ignoring Jonathan's behavior stops these problems," Mrs. Bartlett decided. "Maybe by not giving him the attention he wants, I will show Jonathan that behaving poorly is not worth the trouble and embarrassment it causes him. If I simply ignore Jonathan's behavior maybe his classmates will also or maybe they will show him that they are not impressed by his actions." These resolutions were firm in Mrs. Bartlett's mind as the eighth-graders began pouring into the classroom and chatting noisily away before the beginning of class.

When the bell finally rang, Mrs. Bartlett noticed that Jonathan was not in the room. She started the lecture wondering if he had seized another opportunity to skip class. Just at that moment, Jonathan came into the classroom shutting the door noisily behind him. He swaggered to his seat with a smug expression on his face. Mrs. Bartlett swallowed her desire to ask him the reason for his tardiness and continued with her lesson. However, it was difficult for her to concentrate as she glanced to the back of the room where Jonathan was slouching in his seat with a tired, pouty look on his sallow face. Despite the thin blond hair that was falling over Jonathan's forehead, Mrs. Bartlett could see the distant look in his pale blue eyes. She sighed to herself thinking, "I want to ignore Jonathan's poor behavior, not Jonathan himself." From that point on, Mrs. Bartlett tried to draw Jonathan into the conversation about the latest literary selection that had read in class. However, he did not want to be asked any questions or included in the discussion at all. In fact, Mrs. Bartlett's attention achieved the opposite effect of what she had hoped for. Jonathan began irritating the other students around him and making wise-cracks about the people in the class who were interested in the discussion. The class became so disrupted that Mrs. Bartlett could not continue with her lesson. Just as she decided that it was time to stop the problems Jonathan was causing, the bell rang signifying the end of the period and the students began rushing to their lockers to prepare for the next class.

That evening at home, Mrs. Bartlett pondered over what her best course of action would be in dealing with Jonathan. She had been coping with his behavior problems and his sulky attitude since school had begun four weeks ago. Talking to Jonathan alone about modifying his actions had not helped at all. In fact, it had only made things worse. Correcting him in front of his peers, and sending him to the dean had not helped solve the situation either because he enjoyed being in the spotlight and receiving attention from everyone. "What should I do?" Mrs. Bartlett fretted. "Should I send him back to the dean where he will probably receive corporal punishment this time, or should I arrange a conference with Jonathan's parents to see if their intervention could help him improve the situation?"

What is pre-service candidates' analysis of the case? How does their analysis compare with that of the school faculty analysis which follows?

School Faculty Analysis: Case 9

Carol Bregman, Rebecca Francis, Cynthia Lasky, Mariolga Lebredo, Bertha Moro, Judy Newman, Doris Olesky, Mickey Weiner

Case Analysis

Step 1: Elements of the Problem

The school faculty notes the following elements in the case: (a) lack of student motivation (b) classroom management (c) student behavior and attitudes and (d) a disruptive learning environment.

Step 2: Identifying the Facts in the Case

The group perceives the following facts in the case:

1. Mrs. Bartlett has been dealing with behavior problems instigated by Jonathan in her fifth period English class for four weeks.
2. Jonathan is frequently tardy and disruptive in class.
3. Mrs. Bartlett has tried various strategies to engage Jonathan's attention and improve his behavior yet none has as of yet been effective.
4. At times, Mrs. Bartlett's class has become so disruptive that she could not continue with her lesson.
5. Mrs. Bartlett has sent Jonathan to the dean for his misbehavior and she is contemplating calling his parents to help improve the situation.

Step 3: Understanding the Problem

The group sees the following as having a bearing on the case even though not stated explicitly in the case:

1. Why has Mrs. Bartlett only used "mild" attempts to confront Jonathan's behavior? Is this her philosophy? Has she ever used a stricter or harsher approach? Has she observed that any of the strategies she has tried have made a difference in his behavior?

2. Why does Jonathan crave attention? Perhaps he likes being the class clown and being popular with the other students. Maybe Jonathan lacks attention at home or is neglected by his parents. There may be some problem in the home that he is attempting to "escape" through his behavior.

3. Does Jonathan frequently arrive late to class? This may be a major factor in the onset of his behavior problem. Mrs. Bartlett may want to inquire why he is often tardy. Is there a good reason, or is he late on purpose?

4. Why is Jonathan pouting, and why does he have a sallow face with a distant look in his eyes? Perhaps Jonathan lacks sleep or has a difficult home life that is traumatic for him.

5. Has Mrs. Bartlett attempted to find out Jonathan's interests and/or talents? Perhaps, she could focus on that or assist him in developing these areas or relate it to what she is teaching so he would be more interested in classroom activities.

6. Is this the only class in which Jonathan has problems? Perhaps Mrs. Bartlett can discuss her problems with Jonathan's behavior with other teachers and obtain their suggestions and recommendations.

7. Is Jonathan a loner except for his acting out in class? Perhaps, he is lonely and has no friends and this is his attempt at reaching out.

8. How is Jonathan performing academically? Is it possible that he is either bored or frustrated and therefore chooses to act out for attention?

9. On how many occasions, if any, has Mrs. Bartlett contacted Jonathan's family? What were the outcomes of each communication?

Step 3: Relevant Knowledge Base

The group notes that answers to the foregoing issues is predicated upon one having a sound knowledge of the following ideas/concepts, etc.:

- Relationship between classroom behavior and attitudes toward learning.
- Attendance/tardy policy of the school.
- Motivation.

- Family background.
- Managing student conduct.
- Conflict resolution.
- Peer collaboration.
- Parent conferencing/ family involvement.

Step 4: Finding Assumptions

The school faculty identifies the following things taken for granted in the case:

- Off-task behavior of a student can disrupt his own learning and that of other students. The group finds this assumption to be valid based on professional experience.
- A teacher's behavior (such as ignoring misconduct) can influence a student's behavior. The group finds this assumption to be valid in many but not all cases.
- Lecture is an appropriate method of instruction for an 8th grade English class. The group finds this assumption to be valid in some cases and invalid in others and hopes that the teacher varies the means of instruction no matter what grade or subject is being taught.
- All students deserve opportunities to learn. It is the professional judgment of the group that this is a valid assumption.
- There is more than one method of managing student misconduct. The group finds validity in this assumption based on professional experience.
- Teachers have a responsibility to send severely disruptive students to the dean. The group finds this assumption to be valid in some but not all cases.
- Parent communication and intervention can improve a student's classroom behavior. The group finds this assumption to be valid in some cases and not valid in other instances.

Step 5: Detecting Arguments

The group identified the following arguments in the case:

- Dealing with a behavior problem for many weeks using the same approach does not correct the behavior problem.

Mrs. Bartlett has been using the same approach for many weeks to deal with Jonathan's behavior problem; therefore, that is why Jonathan's behavior problem persists. The group finds that this argument does not follow (*non-sequitur*).

- Lectures are not a motivating form of instruction for students who have behavior problems. Jonathan has behavior problems; therefore, he is not motivated during Mrs. Bartlett's lectures. The group finds that this argument commits the four-term fallacy.

- When a teacher contacts parents regarding a student's behavior, the student's behavior improves. Mrs. Bartlett decides to contact Jonathan's parents; therefore, Jonathan's behavior will improve. According to the school faculty, this arguments begs the question.

- Teachers should remove disruptive students from their learning environment. Jonathan is a disruptive student; therefore, he should be removed from Mrs. Bartlett's learning environment. This argument does not follow according to the group.

- When a student is sent to the dean, his learning process is disrupted. Jonathan was sent to the dean; therefore, his learning process was disrupted. While the hypothetical structure of the argument is valid (affirming the antecedent), the group finds that the argument begs the question regarding the causes of a student's learning process being disrupted.

- Students who display disruptive behavior in school are lacking attention. Jonathan displays disruptive behavior in school; therefore, Jonathan lacks attention. The finds that this argument also begs the question.

- Students disrupt the class when they are bored. Jonathan disrupts Mrs. Bartlett's class; therefore Jonathan is bored in her class. According to the group, this argument does not follow.

Step 6: Interpretation of the Case

Mrs. Bartlett is having trouble dealing with Jonathan's attitudes and behavior in her classroom. She has tried a number of strategies such as speaking with him privately, correcting his misbehavior, ignoring his misbehavior, redirecting his attention back to the learning activity, and sending him to the dean. However, his behavior has not improved and he continues to be disruptive not only to himself but to the class.

One thing that does seem clear from this case is that Mrs. Bartlett wants to reach and teach Jonathan. She has tried a variety of strategies rather than immediately sending him out of the room, as her teacher's contract may enable her to do when he disrupts the learning environment of the class. She has spent some time reflecting on what she feels may help Jonathan even though she may not know what to try next. One may wonder if Mrs. Bartlett has thought about collaborating with other teachers or faculty members who could perhaps help her by sharing new ideas or approaches which may improve her situation with Jonathan.

It is not clear from this case why Mrs. Bartlett has let four weeks go by before deciding to contact Jonathan's family. Tolerating misbehavior for four weeks may send a message to students that the behavior is acceptable classroom behavior. One wonders if during the four weeks Mrs. Bartlett attempted in any way to work with Jonathan to determine what the cause(s) of the misbehavior may have been. Also, it was stated at the end of the case that Mrs. Bartlett chose to send Jonathan to the dean before she considered calling his family, when often teachers may wish to try to work with the student and his family before seeking administrative intervention unless the violation of the code of student conduct is severe. It is not clear, however, if she has had previous communication with Jonathan's family and what the results of the prior contact may have been.

In addition to Jonathan's misbehavior, the teacher is also struggling with his attitude. One wonders if the teacher or counselor has made any attempt to encourage the student to examine his own beliefs about school or behavior or to identify why he is misbehaving. Have the teacher, counselor or other students participated in any sort of group discussion at which time attitudes and their relationship to behaviors could be examined? According to Ruggiero (2000), confronting attitudes that hinder learning can be done once the beliefs or attitudes are identified and accessible to logical analysis. Jonathan as well as other students could perhaps benefit by becoming aware of healthy and unhealthy attitudes that impact motivation, classroom behavior and learning.

Perhaps one reason students sometimes misbehave or exhibit negative attitudes toward school is because they see little or no purpose or relevance between the course content and their lives. Mrs. Bartlett can learn from Jonathan, for example, about his hobbies, or a possible career choice he might enjoy pursuing in his future.

Mrs. Bartlett can link her instruction to Jonathan's world and help him see connections between the content she is teaching and his future. Since she is an English teacher, it does not seem overly difficult to connect the importance of communication either through writing, reading, listening or speaking to any goal Jonathan may have for himself. If Jonathan is able to see relevance or a purpose or make a personal connection with his class work, he may become more motivated to want to learn and his behavior and attitudes may, therefore, improve.

Solution(s)

- Mrs. Bartlett may benefit by collaborating with other teachers, the counselor or Jonathan's friends and family to identify why Jonathan is choosing to misbehave. Even though she has tried several different approaches, if she feels that her methods have not worked she can consult with others to help her improve her ability to help Jonathan. She can also talk with other students in the class who may be Jonathan's friends and ask them for their assistance in getting Jonathan to focus and become more involved in the learning process. Perhaps, if Jonathan is encouraged by his peers, he will be more likely to positively change his behavior.

- Mrs. Bartlett may wish to contact Jonathan's parents. His family may not be aware that Jonathan is having problems in school and can support Mrs. Bartlett in reaching Jonathan. Consistent communication with parents may be able to help keep Jonathan's behavior in check. Mrs. Bartlett may also become aware of Jonathan's home situation and problems there that may help explain his behavior. She may wish to confer with Jonathan's family as to whether or not they would like him to have a mentor or a Big Brother who can work with him on a regular basis.

- Mrs. Bartlett might try to help Jonathan explore his interests and talents so that she can focus on his strengths and in doing so, motivate Jonathan to become more involved in his learning process. Relating Jonathan's interests and talents to class instruction can perhaps motivate Jonathan to become more interested in the class.

- Mrs. Bartlett may be able to reach Jonathan by letting him know that someone is interested in helping him develop his talents. If his talents and interests can be used to improve his attitudes toward school, perhaps he will wish to arrive to class on time and with a renewed spirit toward learning. Perhaps Jonathan will be more likely to display positive attitudes and good behavior if he feels he has special talents which he can share with the class.
- Mrs. Bartlett may want to attend some workshops to update her knowledge on classroom management techniques, conflict resolution, peer mediation and maybe even teaching approaches which rely less heavily on lecture as the primary means for delivery of instruction.

Case 10

Mr. Goodall, the elementary school principal, looked up when he heard a knock on his door. It was Mrs. Williams, one of his fifth grade teachers. She was twenty minutes early for a scheduled appointment with the principal and the parents of a handicapped student of hers.

"I know I'm early, but I wanted to talk to you in private before Mike's parents arrived. May I come in?" asked Mrs. Williams nervously.

"Of course," said Mr. Goodall, "What did you want to talk to me about?" Even as he asked the question, Mr. Goodall knew the problems that Mrs. Williams had been having with Mike, a handicapped student that had been mainstreamed into Mrs. Williams classroom. The meeting this afternoon between the school and the parents was to decide whether or not Mike should be changed to another classroom.

"Mr. Goodall, I know how you feel about changing children to other classrooms, and I know this is a practice that you don't like to do, but I just feel as though Mike is not receiving the appropriate help he needs in my classroom. I want to suggest to his parents that he be moved into Mr. Downs' room where he can be with other children with special needs."

Mr. Goodall sighed. "You know how Mike's parents feel about that. They want Mike to be around children of his own age, without putting him in special classes anymore. They have the legal right to have him placed in the least restrictive environment. Mr. Downs' classroom is for learning disabled and emotionally handicapped children. Mike is neither of those; he is simply confined to a wheelchair because of a crippling childhood illness. I was hoping that after a six week period, you would get used to the slight inconveniences of having Mike in your classroom."

"Slight inconveniences!" gasped Mrs. Williams, "I can hardly concentrate on anyone except Mike. He is a disturbance to the entire class. I have my classroom set up in learning centers, as you know, and Mike cannot get around to the centers without my help or that of at least two students. He has a hard time getting supplies such as books, learning games and math puzzles. I have already rearranged my entire room to accommodate Mike. I have moved everything into his reach in hopes that he might try and help himself, but he still relies on me or other students to fetch him whatever he needs."

"I will agree that Mike is somewhat spoiled," said Mr. Goodall, "but this does not give us the legal or the moral right to change him to another classroom. I chose you to take on Mike because of your excellent record with all of your other students. You have always been able to manage a classroom and your students have always excelled. This inclusion of Mike is a pilot program in our school. He is the first handicapped student that has come to Brownsville Elementary. We received the funds for the appropriate modifications such as bathrooms, ramps, and even an elevator. We must work together to sort out whatever problems Mike is causing in the classroom and make this program a success."

"I agree this program is important, but what about the other students? Is it fair that I devote the majority of my time to helping one student? I don't even know if I can give Mike the kind of help a boy in a wheelchair needs. Sometimes he gets so frustrated he starts shaking his head back and forth and no one can calm him down."

Just then Mike's parents, Mr, and Mrs. Ball arrived for their appointment. They are both aware of the problem that Mike has been having in Mrs. Williams' classroom, and hope to get these problems resolved. They had previously sent Mike to a very expensive school for the handicapped, but felt that he would benefit more in a regular school environment. Mike never had many friends, and the Balls hoped that Mike would do better socially in his new school.

"Please come in and make yourselves comfortable," said Mr. Goodall pleasantly. "I'm glad that you could make it today to discuss your son's progress after the first six weeks in his new school. First of all, are there any questions that you may have?"

"Well, Mike seems to be doing Ok," stated Mrs. Ball, "but quite frankly he complains that Mrs. Williams seems to pick on him. He says that she puts him in the back of the classroom a lot and does not let him participate in many of the activities in which the other children take part."

"I can explain that," said Mrs. Williams calmly. "I don't pick on Mike, but I do have to spend quite a bit of time keeping him from talking to others and staying on task. Sometimes the rest of the class is working independently on projects that I don't feel Mike is ready for yet, so I put him in the back of the class where I feel he can be most comfortable working on areas such as his math skills in which I feel he needs reinforcement."

"Mike feels as though you think he can't do the same work as the other students. We want him to learn to do the same kind of activities as the rest of his classmates. Otherwise, he will never be able to survive in the real world or make friends who respect him for who he is," Mr. Ball said slowly. "If he is any kind of discipline problem to the class, then that is something new to us. Mike has always been a great kid who is easy to get along with. Maybe he senses that he is being discriminated against because of his handicap."

"I have to disagree with that," said Mr. Goodall. "Mrs. Williams is a grade A teacher, and I know she would never discriminate against any student because of a handicap. This is the first time our school has had a student in a wheelchair, but I can honestly say I don't know of any faculty member, including Mrs. Williams, who would discriminate against Mike because of his handicap. Everyone is more than willing to work with him and help him in any way they can."

"When I first came to this meeting, I felt that I could not have Mike in my classroom anymore because I thought I could not give him the kind of attention he needed. Mike talks out in class too much, expects things immediately, and portrays an attitude that he is the most important student in the class. I realize he has always been given special attention, but as his teacher, I feel he must be taught that if he wants to be treated like others, then he must follow the same courtesies the other students are expected to extend," Mrs. Williams said hesitantly. "Perhaps, we should have a meeting with Mike and go over some of the problems we are having. I feel this is a difficult period of adjustment for the entire class, and we will all have to sort things out to make this work."

"I will agree that Mike can be difficult at times, probably because we have always treated him special," said Mrs. Ball. "That is why we feel it is so important that Mike learn the appropriate social skills he will need to function in society. Academically, is he having any problems?"

"He is still somewhat slow at picking up his math skills," Mrs. Williams stated, "but basically Mike is a bright intelligent 5th grader. If he would be a little more patient, I could incorporate him into more of the learning centers. I feel he would benefit in working cooperatively with the other children, but he must get rid of his attitude that the class is just for him. Do you think you could talk to him about this?"

"Yes," agreed Mrs. Ball, "We will work on this. I know that Mike can be impatient and gets frustrated easily. I think this is a big adjustment for him to be around so many other students also."

She noted, "The private institution he went to only had six other students in the class, and there were two teachers."

"If we talk to Mike, will you be willing to still have him in your classroom?" asked Mrs. Ball.

"Of course I would!" exclaimed Mrs. Williams. I would also like both of you to visit Mike in the classroom and offer me any suggestions you have to make things for Mike easier to get to or be more comfortable."

"Well I guess this about wraps up our first meeting together. I suggest that we all get together in another six weeks to evaluate Mike's progress. If you should have any problems or questions prior to that meeting, please feel free to call me or Mrs. Williams," said Mr. Goodall.

Mr. and Mrs. Ball thanked Mr. Goodall and Mrs. Williams and left.

"Well, do you feel any better?" asked Mr. Goodall.

"Yes, I really do hope things work out. I would like to have Mike in my classroom, I just worry about the other students also. I felt like Mike was taking up too much of my time with his needs and special attention. Maybe things will get better after his parents talk to him. They seem to really care about the situation. I'll let you know if I have any more problems."

"You are a great teacher Mrs. Williams," Mr. Goodall said. "I have all the faith in the world you will make it work. Thank you."

What is pre-service candidates' analysis of the case? How does their analysis compare with that of the school faculty analysis which follows?

School Faculty Analysis: Case 10

Carol Bregman,, Rebecca Francis, Cynthia Lasky, Mariolga Lebredo, Berth Moro, Judy Newman, Doris Olesky, Mickey Weiner

Case Analysis

Step 1: Elements of the Problem

The school faculty concludes that the following are elements in the case: (a) funding and pressures involved in a pilot program (b) mainstreaming/inclusion/ESE (c) labels (LD, EH, Physically Handicapped) (d) physical/social/emotional needs of learners (e) attitudes/adjustments to a new program for teachers and students (f) parent communication (g) learned helplessness (spoiled child) (h) support of administration (i) private vs. public school expectations (j) cooperative group work and (k) building a community of learners.

Step 2: Identifying the Facts in the Case

The group points to the following facts in the case:

1. Mrs. Williams, a fifth grade teacher, had scheduled a meeting with her principal, Mr. Goodall, and the parents of Mike, a handicapped student recently mainstreamed into her class.
2. Mr. Goodall and Mike's parents were aware of Mrs. Williams' problems with Mike.
3. The conference was to decide whether Mike should be changed to another classroom or remain with Mrs. Williams' class.
4. Mrs. Williams felt Mike was not receiving the appropriate help he needs in her classroom.
5. Mike's parents want him to be around children his age, without being in special classes. Though Mike is confined to a wheelchair, he is not emotionally handicapped, nor does he have a learning disability..
6. Mrs. Williams feels Mike is a disturbance to the entire class. Her class set up in learning centers and Mike cannot get around without help.

7. Even though Mrs. Williams has rearranged her classroom and moved everything within Mike's reach, Mike still relies on others to get him what he needs.

8. Mike is the first handicapped student at Brownsville Elementary. His inclusion into Mrs. William's class is a pilot program.

9. The school has received funding to make appropriate modifications to accommodate Mike.

10. Mike had been previously sent to a very expensive private school for the handicapped but now his parents felt he'd benefit more in a regular school environment.

11. Mrs. Williams invited Mike's parents to visit the classroom and give her suggestions.

12. Mr. Goodall suggested everyone get together again in six weeks to evaluate Mike's progress.

Step 3:   Understanding the Problem

The school faculty indicates that the following have a bearing on the case even though they are not stated explicitly in the case:

1. Is Mike also having problems in his special area classes (i.e., music, art, P.E., etc.)? If so, Mrs. Williams may want to discuss this with these teachers to get their input and support, especially in communicating her concerns with the principal and parents.

2. Is there a reason Mrs. Williams doesn't have an aide? Having an aide would help her deal with Mike in the classroom and facilitate the situation by giving Mike more individual attention. Perhaps, she can inquire whether the funding given for the pilot program to mainstream Mike into her classroom would pay for an aide.

3. Do Mike's parents give him chores to do or responsibilities at home? If they don't and "cater" to his every need and want, he may be expecting the same kind of treatment in school. If they do, then there is no reason why Mrs. Williams can't expect him to be more self-reliant in the classroom.

4. Is Mike purposely acting more helpless than he really is? If he is, this may indicate he wants attention or has developed a pattern and has gotten used to people catering to him.

5. Has Mrs. Williams received complaints or heard concerns of other parents of other students in the classroom regarding Mike?

If she has, she may be feeling more pressure to solve this problem.   If parents feel Mike is taking up too much of Mrs. Williams time and it's affecting their children's progress, she may be concerned about this and future actions these parents may take.

6. Does Mike have any special hobbies or interests?   Perhaps allowing him to share these with the class would make him feel more confident and independent.

7. Is Mike involved in any other activities outside of school? If he is this may help him in developing his social skills and in gaining independence to do things for himself.

8. Does Mike have any jobs or responsibilities in the classroom? If so, he may tend to feel more responsible and needed by others and therefore, be more willing to help himself.

9. Which school, public or private, does Mike prefer?   Why? Knowing this may help Mike reflect on why he may be finding it difficult to adjust to a different environment.

Step 3: Relevant Knowledge Base

The group motes that answers to the foregoing issues is predicated upon one having a sound knowledge (theoretical, empirical, craft wisdom, content) of the following concepts/ideas:

- Accommodating individual differences in learning.
- Inclusion.
- Learner Equity.
- Parental involvement.
- Cooperative groups.
- Collaborative problem solving.

Step 4: Finding Assumptions

The group notes that the following are taken for granted in the case:

- Handicapped students may have special needs. The group finds this assumption to be valid but notes that all students may have special needs.

- Handicapped students can be successful in a regular classroom. The group finds this assumption to be valid based on professional knowledge and experience.
- Communicating with parents can enhance a child's learning process. The group finds this assumption to be valid based on professional knowledge.
- Supportive parents can contribute to a child's success in school. The group finds this assumption to be valid.
- Students can learn to work in cooperative groups. The group finds this assumption to be true based on classroom experience, but notes that simply placing students in groups does not mean that the group will be successful.
- Teachers working with handicapped students may need special training. The group finds this assumption to be valid as special assistance or support is sometimes needed.
- Teachers should be concerned about all the students in their classroom getting an equal opportunity to learn. The group finds this assumption to be valid and recognizes that the assumption is based on classroom realities.
- Handicapped students can become independent and self-reliant. The group finds this assumption to be true based on professional knowledge and classroom experience.

Step 5: Detecting Arguments

The school faculty points to the following arguments in the case:

- Handicapped students have special needs. Mike is a handicapped student; therefore, he has special needs. This argument is valid according to the school faculty.
- Handicapped students can benefit from being mainstreamed. Mike is a handicapped student; therefore he will benefit from being mainstreamed. The group also finds this argument to be valid.
- Physically handicapped students have different needs than other handicapped students. Mike is a physically handicapped student; therefore, his needs are different than those of other handicapped students who are not physically impaired. This group sees this argument as valid.

- Students can learn to work in cooperative groups. Mike is a student; therefore, he can learn to work cooperatively with others. The group finds that the structure of this categorical syllogism to be valid.
- Teachers who work with handicapped students need special training. Mrs. Williams has a handicapped student in her classroom; therefore, she needs special training. This argument is valid according to the group.
- Students must assume responsibilities in the classroom community of learners. Mike is a student; therefore, he must assume responsibility in his classroom. The group also finds this argument to be valid.
- Handicapped students should observe the same classroom courtesies as other students. Mike is a handicapped student; therefore, he should observe the same classroom courtesies as other students in his class. The school faculty finds this to be a valid argument.
- Students benefit when parents support their educational program and communicate with the school. Mike's parents support his educational program and communicate with the school; therefore, Mike benefits. The group finds this argument to be circular.

Step 6: Interpretation of Case

During a conference, a classroom teacher and the parents of a physically handicapped fifth grade student who is confined to a wheelchair share their concerns regarding the best placement for the child. At the beginning of the conference the teacher expressed concerns about the student's behaviors and attitudes. She believed that her classroom may not be the best placement for the student for two main reasons: (1) she could not provide the time or resources she felt he required and (2) as she tried to spend the extra time with him that he needed, the needs of the other students in the class would not be met.

On the other hand, Mike's parents expressed their concerns that Mike feels picked on when he is singled out to go to the back of the room and excluded from ongoing classroom activities. As the conference progressed, the teacher seemed more able to want to understand Mike and his needs while his parents seemed to want to understand the teacher's classroom observations and her professional opinion.

Different perspectives were shared openly since the tone of the conference was not hostile. Both the teacher and the student's family were able to communicate freely about their expectations, decisions and concerns until finally some common ground was found: Mike, the student, deserves opportunities to succeed, as do all children, and that the responsibility for providing a successful experience lies not only on the teacher, school and family but also on Mike, himself. The conference ended on a positive note at which time all parties agreed that the best place for Mike was to remain in Mrs. William's classroom.

Throughout the conference, the presence of a supportive administrator was felt as he listened to both sides of the question, "Where is the best placement for Mike?" Regardless of whether the principal had any intention of switching Mike's classroom, his democratic rather than authoritarian leadership style facilitated the meeting and may have contributed a sense of empowerment to his teacher since her voice and concerns were being heard and respected (Maeroff, 1988). Mike's parents may have also felt validated since their concerns regarding what is best for their child were being discussed in a caring and collaborative environment.

It is interesting to note that Mike's parents reported that Mike was feeling discriminated against when he was excluded from certain classroom activities. Similarly, perhaps Mrs. Williams felt discriminated against, of sorts, when she was selected to be the teacher who received a physically handicapped student in her class. Even though the principal explained that he selected her to pilot the mainstreaming program because he had no doubt that she could handle Mike and any special needs he may have, other teachers may not interpret this gesture as an honor. In fact, what it can actually become is additional paperwork and responsibilities piled atop what may seem to be an already insurmountable workload.

One may wonder from this case what sorts of preparation the teacher or other students had as to how, or if, life in the classroom would change with the addition of a new friend who happens to need a wheelchair to get from place to place. Were the students aware that the school is piloting a new program? Was there any group discussion about mainstreaming or inclusion? Perhaps a rap session on labeling could have been conducted by either the counselor or teacher or even Mike's family, at which time all students could be asked to share labels that they, too, have worn at one time or another.

During the discussion, students could be guided to the conclusion that labels come from an external environment but on the inside human beings have similar needs. Discussing how a physical handicap does not necessarily limit one's ability to learn may have benefited Mike who would now know that the teacher and students believe in him and have high expectations for all learners to try their best in all classroom activities.

If Mike is aware that the teacher and students expect him to be a fully contributing member of the classroom family, his learned helplessness or expectation that others should wait on him might disappear. Moreover, when teachers spend time building a sense of community in the classroom by letting students share experiences which are common to other members in the class, holistic connections with one's inner self and other individuals can be fostered (Suhor, 1998). If classmates focus on noting the commonalities (being in 5th grade, wanting to make friends...) rather than the differences (wheelchair, physical handicap...) which exist between and among members in the classroom, much of the fear associated with the unknown or being different can be reduced or even removed. In this way, one can see how a positive classroom climate capitalizing on courtesy and respect for all learners could more easily be developed.

Undoubtedly, Mike is having to undergo many adjustments since he now attends a public school with many more students and fewer adults in the classroom to help him. However, a group discussion during which time the words "transition" or "adjustment" are explored might allow all students to remember various moves or adjustments that each of them has had to make. The pros and cons of Mike's move from his former private school to his present classroom could be highlighted so that Mike and all the other learners would become more familiar with concepts related to change, a natural experience for all learners.

Once learners identify that everyone has and will continue to make transitions and adjustments to new settings and situations as a natural part of becoming lifelong learners, children may relish opportunities to work with each other and celebrate both the similarities and differences of their own personal experience.

This case illustrates how collaborative efforts between a family and a school, including administrators, teachers, families and students, can most certainly contribute to understanding problems and developing solutions. What a grand conclusion to our case study experience!

Solution(s)

- Mrs. Williams may wish to find out more about what funds are available for this pilot program to mainstream Mike. Perhaps there is money to hire an aide to help her with Mike's needs in the classroom, or there is money available to purchase special supplies, equipment or materials (i.e., teacher resources, or workshops to train teachers who feel they would benefit and become more able to successfully work with handicapped students).
- Mrs. Williams may wish to educate herself in the special needs of handicapped students. She may be able to get assistance from an ESE teacher at her school or from another school that services handicapped students. Mrs. Williams may want to consider taking a class on meeting the diverse needs of exceptional students, for example, or "Mainstreaming/Inclusion Made Easy." The more information and knowledge she acquires, the better prepared she may feel to work with a physically handicapped student.
- Mrs. Williams might need to maintain consistent and frequent communication with Mike's parents. The more she informs them of his progress and requests their assistance and support, the more Mike and all the students will benefit.
- Adjusting to a new program takes time, and Mrs. Williams will have to go through an adjustment period in working with Mike. The support of other teachers and the administration is essential, and she might choose to seek their assistance when necessary. Regular meetings with Mr. Goodall to keep him informed of Mike's progress is essential, as well as meetings with the parents to assess and evaluate Mike's progress.
- Perhaps Mrs. Williams can team Mike up with another student in the class to not only help Mike with his math or academic skills but also to build social skills by working cooperatively with a learning buddy. As Mike feels more accepted, he might be more willing to work cooperatively with others because he will feel more self-confident and able to contribute to the group's learning process.
- Mrs. Williams might decide to spend some time to develop a community of learners in her classroom.

School Faculty Reflections: Reflecting on the Problem Solving Process in a Learning Community

The following is the school faculty's reflection on the process of its collaboration and problem solving in case analysis:

We found the collaboration process extremely powerful. It heightened our thinking past the initial response, making us look deep into past experiences, beliefs, and knowledge. It brought a special bond with colleagues, giving a level of trust and admiration where what we said and thought were truly an authentic part of the process of analysis. Each one of us came with different perspectives that added to the whole. There were no right nor wrong answers, just the process of critical thinking. We came together because we care for children, teachers, and each other and wanted to do the best we could for all. We became our students: we learned from each other, and took all the pieces to make a better whole.

There was a definite advantage in working together collaboratively to analyze the cases. Our diverse view points as individuals with varied ethnic backgrounds, and coming from different regions of the country, enriched the experience. The combined accumulation of years of teaching experience, our different experiences as teachers of art, pre-kindergarten, primary and intermediate levels, as well as in gifted education, provided us with a wide variety of educational perspectives.

Our case study group participants' varied ages, years of teaching and experiences provided a road map for looking at each case and arriving at solutions. Our different experiences and perspectives also enhanced the process by providing a combination of various ideas, rather than one single view point. We pulled from each other's backgrounds and experiences to analyze the cases and successfully go through the steps of problem solving.

We, ourselves, became primary resources from which we could solve the problems in the cases. We found the process of collaboration to be extremely powerful. It heightened our awareness and thinking process past initial responses, making us look deeper into past personal experiences, beliefs and knowledge.

The problem solving process raised our thinking to a higher level, as the problem solving steps allowed us to really dissect all of the elements of the problem in arriving at effective solutions in each case.

The socialization aspect of the collaboration and problem solving process was very enjoyable and personally satisfying for all group participants. We met at our various domains, where we were able to interact with each other on a more personal basis.

We initially came together because we care for children, teachers, and each other. We desired to do the best we could for all involved. As we developed a feeling of comaraderie and friendship, we looked forward to discussing our feelings and sharing tasks. In the end, this special group developed a greater respect and admiration for each other as professionals, as we learned of each other's gifts and talents which contributed to the overall success of our collaborative experience. We became our own students, as we learned from each other and put all of the pieces together to make a better whole.

Implications for Practice

The school faculty's experience certainly reaffirms the recent findings about the social nature of learning vis-à-vis learning communities. The case analysis process, according to the foregoing lived-experience, seems to enhance learning. This form of learning seems to occur through participation as the school faculty engaged in common activity. The learning happened between and among members of the group. According to the National Institute on Educational Governance, Finance, Policy Making, and Management (1998):

> [This form of learning] assumes that *knowledge is distributed* among members in any group and the work should be organized to draw upon their collective expertise.... Optimal learning experiences happen when participants work in their *zone of proximal development*: a level above their performance capabilities when working alone, but within their reach when working collaboratively with more expert assistance (1).

The school faculty makes a cogent plea for more opportunities for school practitioners and pre-service teacher education candidates to enjoy this form of learning and knowledge acquisition:

At a time when education is being questioned, and the performance of teachers and students is constantly being evaluated as if in a "fishbowl" for onlookers to constantly critique, the collaborative experience can present a refreshing alternative for teachers, administrators, parents and community members. Since collaboration promotes a sense of ownership and belonging for participants, those who are involved in the process can feel more satisfaction and responsibility for decisions made.

As the pressures on teachers and school systems increase, collaboration may be the only solution that will provide a new way of looking at current educational issues for the benefit of all involved. Now a days, teachers are feeling more and more frustrated in that they are being required to teach to prepare students to excel on standardized tests. Legislators, the community and school board members seem to have come to the conclusion that students are only learning if they do well on standardized tests. Other factors that effect learning are being put aside to concentrate on increasing standardized test scores.

Teachers have become like "robots" that are programmed to teach a curriculum that teaches their students how to take and do well on tests. A teacher's autonomy in making curriculum decisions has all but disappeared, as has the teacher's right to select appropriate teaching strategies to enhance learning, as well as to creatively use his/her professional expertise.

How can the collaboration process and experience play an important role in putting educational decision-making back into the hands of the teacher? Well, for starters, collaboration brings about a variety of opinions and experiences to evaluate and critique. New ways of looking at an issue can arise as educators come together to share their view points. Coming together as individuals for the good of the whole, not only promotes team work and bonding, but also provides a means for validating personal feelings and knowledge.

Collaborative teams can create positive results. If school faculties are given the opportunity to meet collaboratively, the chances of ideas and solutions derived from these meetings effectively enhancing the learning process for students is much greater. When one is allowed to express his/her thoughts and insights, one feels more committed and responsible to the cause at hand.

Collaboration needs to expand beyond experienced teachers and extend to include pre-service candidates, administrators, school board members, parents and the community. Collaboration experiences also need to expand into the classroom where students, themselves, can become agents for planning and executing their own learning process to best suit their own cooperative and individual needs. If schools around the county viewed collaboration as important and rewarding as our collaborative group did, the benefits it could provide for all involved would be amazing: the best decisions would be derived, issues would be dissected and resolved, problems would be looked at from all angles.

The learners' needs would be prioritized to be the main issue, and how to most appropriately and adequately meet those needs through the goal of problem-solving.

Convincing those that are far removed from the classroom, but have the power to make educational decisions effecting teachers and students, will be the ultimate challenge. To us, as teachers, who best know the needs of our students, the decision to utilize the collaboration and problem-solving process seems only natural, and what makes the most sense. Perhaps this book, and our experiences and insights can serve as a vehicle to educate those that are constantly criticizing the teaching profession, and allow others to appreciate the motivation, increase in morale and responsible accountability that collaborative efforts provide.

Our case study analysis can provide a road map and examples for solving similar classroom and other educational situations in an efficient and effective manner. By implementing collaboration and problem-solving as the process for arriving at sound and creative educational decisions student learning will be profoundly impacted. Isn't that our ultimate goal? to make decisions that most positively effect our students?

Reflections of the Learning Community's National Board Member

In November of 1999, I became a national board certified teacher. As a result, I have had the opportunity to mentor other national board candidates over the past year. I would, therefore, like to share several connections which exist between the process of national board certification and the problem solving process that was employed as we analyzed the case studies in this book:

- When working on case studies, our group first identified the elements of a problem in order to try to make sense out of the information given. This process of determining what the essential elements are in terms of characters, context, and so on, must be undertaken so that one or more problems can be defined. One is more apt to work towards a solution if the problem is clearly understood.

- Candidates in the national board process must be able to identify learners who present certain challenges or have specific problems before plans can be made to help improve the situation or resolve the problem(s).
- Determining what is known about specific learners and their context, both within and outside of one's classroom, is directly relevant when completing portfolio entries and assessment exercises. That is, candidates must describe the featured student, and share relevant background knowledge regarding the learner's unique characteristics, strengths and weaknesses so that it is clear why the teacher makes decisions which occur in the student's learning environment.
- In our case analysis, we moved from the known facts to the unknown information in the cases. During the national board process, portfolio entries can be thought of as a case study in which the teacher has an opportunity to describe the context of learning (what is known), explain and analyze links between learners and the unit of study, and then reflect on teaching and learning processes and products (what is unknown). The process of moving from what is known to what is not known is also fundamental when completing the assessment center exercises. For example, candidates are given scenarios and asked to address prompts based on a description or situation. Identifying what is known and what information a teacher would want or need to know becomes vital in determining how accomplished practitioners formulate decisions and plans of action.
- Collaboration during the case study analysis helped us identify assumptions in each case. Our study group attempted to determine which assumptions were valid or not valid based on research and/or professional experience. During many phases of the national board process, identifying assumptions in children's development or in learning theory, for example, is beneficial in determining which decisions accomplished teachers should make. The assumption that all students can learn may be valid; but by the same means and at the same pace? The national board certification process also gives teachers an opportunity to identify and reflect on assumptions made in specific learning contexts, and to justify whether assumptions seem valid or invalid.

- Identifying facts, opinions, assumptions and reasoned judgments in order to formulate arguments and draw conclusions was a collaborative process during each case study session. The national board process, as a whole, can be thought of as building a case based on the gathering of documents and artifacts. The teacher determines how to select and organize the artifacts and documents so that they may support thoughtful and competent decisions as well as ethical and professional judgements in defense of accomplished practice. Personnel resources within and outside of the classroom and school community, such as parents, guest speakers, and university professors can become partners in enhancing teaching and learning.
- Collaboration increased our abilities to perceive multiple perspectives and points of view as we worked on the case studies. Similarly, collaborating with colleagues can help national board candidates to be able to identify different angles of a problem and to develop various strategies or identify supplementary resources to help solve the problem. Consulting with colleagues both inside and outside of one's school can be beneficial, and add significantly to one's depth and breadth of understanding.

Learning to Analyze Arguments

There is certainly a clear distinction between simply verifying the accuracy of information and detecting errors in reasoning. For example, one might easily use an historical reference to verify the accuracy of the following events:

1. The "Old Deluder Satan Act" was an educational law enacted in 1647 in Virginia.
2. The first Latin Grammar School in America was established in 1635 in Boston.
3. The first compulsory education law was passed in 1852 in Maryland.
4. The Report of the National Education Association's Committee on the Reorganization of Secondary Education published in 1918 laid out the Seven Cardinal Principles of Secondary Education.

On the other hand, a reference is not very useful in helping one detect fallacies in reasoning in any of the following:

1. Professor: "One should do unto others as she would have them do unto her. If I were a student, I would want to receive an A in this course. Therefore, I should give all my students A's."
2. Lawyer: "Capital punishment is wrong because it is wrong to take a human life."
3. School Principal: "The way to get better teachers is to have teacher candidates take more courses in their subject area."
4. Incumbent Politician: "You wouldn't change surgeons in the middle of an operation. Why change governors in these days of constant crisis."
5. Newspaper Editorial: "Though Clarence Thomas showed little evidence of judicial brilliance in his testimony before the Senate Judiciary Committee, neither did he commit any significant gaffe. Therefore, Thomas should be confirmed as the rightful successor to Justice Thurgood Marshall, the nation's first black Supreme Court justice."

The latter presupposes the use of one's powers of judgment or inference. In other words, the latter requires careful reasoned thinking, that is, being thoughtful. Improving one's judgment, according to the literature on critical thinking, strengthens the link between thinking/thought and action. Reflective teacher education candidates are therefore more prone to display good judgment. Knowing how to make and evaluate inferences is a prerequisite to good thinking and problem solving.

Practicing Good Thinking

Good thinking requires that one will ask critical questions vis-à-vis what one reads, hears, etc. For example, one might ask such questions as, what is the point being made? What arguments are being made and are they valid? Are there assumptions being made that may be invalid? Are there errors in reasoning, that is, informal fallacies being made? (Burton, Kimball & Wing, 1960).

But how does one engage in the process of analyzing what one hears, reads, etc? Is there a process for doing so? For example, suppose one reads the following statement:

Teachers who have been educated in colleges of education are intellectually weak. Bob, the science teacher at Millville High is intellectually sharp. As a result, I am sure he was not educated in a college of education.

The first thing in analyzing what one reads, hears, etc. is to find the author's main point or major conclusion. In this case, the reference to "as a result" suggests a conclusion that follows. In other words, the main conclusion in the statement is that he (Bob) was not educated in a college of education. But how does the author of the statement get to that conclusion? To determine this, one must lay out the structure of the argument. What are the reasons or premises, hidden or explicitly stated, that lead to the conclusion? What inferences are being made or are being suggested? Does the conclusion being offered follow validly from some previous propositions? A closer examination reveals that the author of the statement is offering a conclusion that is supposed to follow from the following propositions:

Proposition 1: Teachers who have been educated in colleges of education are intellectually weak.
Proposition 2: Bob, the science teacher at Millville High, is intellectually sharp.

It seems that the author of the statement is suggesting that propositions 1 and 2 are true and therefore a valid inference might be drawn from these propositions; that inference being that Bob was not educated in a college of education. The form of reasoning seems to be one in which the author of the statement is moving from general premises/propositions that are assumed to be true to a specific conclusion that follows from those premises/propositions. That form of reasoning is known as deductive reasoning and deductive arguments may be analyzed in terms of their form or structure. To do so, one may apply four rules to test the structure of the argument. A prerequisite skill to the foregoing structural analysis of a deductive argument is the ability to standardize sentences into logical forms.

An argument may be defined as a set or series of premises (statements) used to persuade one to accept a particular conclusion. The structure of an argument includes, therefore, the argument's conclusion and its premises. To lay out the structure of a deductive argument, like the foregoing, requires that one first classify the statements in the argument into one of four logical patterns:

All S are P (universal affirmative statement)
No S is P (universal negative statement)
Some S is P (particular affirmative statement)
Some S is not P (particular negative statement).

These categorical forms of statements contain:

(a) a quantifier (all, no, some) that expresses a quantifiable link to the subject of the sentence/statement;
(b) a noun or noun phrase for a subject;
(c) a verb, preferably a form of the infinitive to be; and
(d) a noun or noun phrase for a predicate.

All arguments do not come prepared in one of the four categorical forms but one can find clues through the quantifier.

For example, statements that suggest the following quantifiable references to the subject in the statement may be placed as an ALL statement: every, each, any, always, without exception, or invariably. An if ... then statement may be classified as an ALL statement (e.g., if its an ant then its an insect may be classified as ALL ants are insects). NO statements may be deduced from quantifiable references to: not one, never, not a, under no circumstances, none, not a. SOME ... ARE statements may be deduced from quantifiable references to: there are, several, many, frequently, often, or generally. SOME...ARE NOT statements may be deduced from quantifiable references to: not all and not only. The conversion of a not only statement however requires that one first convert the statement to an ALL statement by reversing the subject and predicate in the statement which follows the word only and then negating that ALL statement. This becomes a SOME ...ARE NOT.

The ability to make inferences enables one to recognize that inferences may be made from a single categorical premise/proposition. For example, a categorical statement NO S is P remains true when reversed NO P is S. A categorical statement SOME S is P remains true when reversed SOME P is S. On the other hand, no valid inference can be made when the following statements are reversed: ALL S is P to ALL P is S, and SOME S is not P to SOME P is not S.

The distribution patterns for the four standard types of categorical propositions may be viewed accordingly:

ALL A is B	SOME A is B
Subject A distributed; Predicate B undistributed	Subject A undistributed; Predicate B undistributed
NO A is B	SOME A is not B
Subject A distributed; Predicate B distributed	Subject A undistributed; Predicate B distributed

The argument that teachers who have been educated in colleges of education are intellectually weak; Bob, the science teacher at Millville High is intellectually sharp; therefore, Bob was not educated in a college of education may be laid out accordingly in categorical proposition form:

ALL S (teachers who have been educated in colleges of education)
are P (people who are intellectually weak);
ALL R (Bob, the science teacher at Millville High) is Q (people who
are intellectually Sharp);
Therefore, NO R (Bob, the science teacher at Millville High) is S (a
teacher who has been educated in a college of education)

But is that categorical structure valid? To determine that, I must use
four rules for checking the validity of a categorical deductive argument.
If the structure fails to meet any of the four rules then it is an invalid
structure. I may say that the structure or form of the argument is
invalid.

Rule 1: a valid categorical deductive argument must have exactly
three terms each used exactly twice to refer to the same class:

ALL S are P
ALL Q are S
Therefore, ALL Q are P.

The term S is the middle or linking term and therefore enables a valid
conclusion (ALL Q are P) to be drawn from the premises ALL S are P
and ALL Q are S.
On the other hand, a categorical deductive argument that contains
more than three terms in the premises cannot lead to any valid
conclusion:

ALL S are P
ALL R are Q
Therefore ALL R is P.

There is no middle or linking term in the premises. So if we take our
foregoing argument and apply rule one we find the following invalid
structure or form:

ALL S (teachers who have been educated in colleges of education)
are P (people who are intellectually weak);
ALL R (Bob, the science teacher at Millville High) is Q
(intellectually sharp); Therefore, NO R (Bob) is S (a teacher educated
in a college of education).

One should note that the structure of the argument contains four terms in the premises. There is no linking term. Consequently, the conclusion cannot be validly drawn from those premises. The argument, therefore, breaks rule one, and commits the **four term fallacy**.

Rule 2: a valid syllogism must have no exclusions or exactly two, one of which must be in the conclusion:

NO S is P
All R is S
Therefore, No R is P.

The form of the above argument shows that in the first premise all of the subject is excluded from the predicate. As a result, one exclusion in either premise must lead to an exclusion in the conclusion. On the other hand, an exclusion in either of the premises that does not lead to an exclusion in the conclusion precipitates a syllogism that contains the **fallacy of faulty exclusion**:

NO S is P
ALL r is S
Therefore ALL R is P.

The form of the argument regarding Bob not being educated in a College of Education does not contain any exclusions and therefore the rule of exclusion is not germane.

Rule 3: in a valid syllogism the middle term must be "distributed" (account in at least one of the reasons/premises in which it occurs for all the members of the class insofar as its relationship to the other class (term) is concerned:

SOME S is P
ALL P is Q
Therefore SOME S is Q.

The foregoing structure highlights the middle term P (the term repeated in the two premises).

The third rule for analyzing the structures of deductive syllogistic arguments requires that in one of the two premises the term P (the middle term) be "distributed" that is it must make reference to all of the things in that category. If the middle term does not then the **fallacy of undistributed middle** is committed:

SOME S is P
SOME Q is P
Therefore SOME Q is S.

Since there is no middle term in the argument regarding Bob the science teacher not being educated in a College of Education then the fallacy of undistributed middle is not relevant.

Rule 4: in a valid categorical deductive argument every term "distributed" in the conclusion must be "distributed" in the premise in which it appears:

ALL P is S
NO S is Q
Therefore NO Q is P.

Note that the terms in the conclusion subject term Q and predicate term P refer to everything in each category. Consequently, the rule requires that in the first premise the term P must be "distributed," which it is, and in the second premise the term Q must be "distributed," which it also is. On the other hand, if a categorical deductive argument's form fails to meet this test then it commits the **fallacy of illicit distribution**:

ALL S is P
NO Q is S
Therefore NO Q is P.

Again the form of the deductive argument regarding Bob the science teacher shows that the subject term in the conclusion that is "distributed" is also "distributed" in the second premise.

However, the form of the argument fails to meet one of the rules and commits the **four term fallacy**. As a result, the form of the argument is invalid. That is, there is a structural defect in the form of the argument.

Hypothetical Deductive Forms

Another form of deductive argument is known as the hypothetical deductive form. In this form, a general connection is made between an antecedent and a consequent and one of four patterns then derived:

Pattern 1: affirming the antecedent
If A then B, A is affirmed, therefore B follows.

If, for example, there is convincing evidence to show that If one is educated in a college of education one is intellectually weak, and we know that Bob, the science teacher was educated in a College of Education, then we may conclude validly that Bob is probably intellectually weak.

Pattern 2: denying the antecedent
If A then B, A is denied, therefore it follows that B is denied.

If, there is convincing evidence to show a sound relationship between persons educated in a college of education and those persons being intellectually weak, and we find that Bob, the science teacher was not educated in a college of education, the invalid conclusion to draw is that Bob is not intellectually weak. He may or may not be intellectually weak. However, that conclusion may not be drawn validly from this form of reasoning.

Pattern 3: denying the consequent
If A then B, B is denied, therefore it follows that A is denied.

If there is convincing evidence to show a sound relationship between persons educated in a college of education and those persons being intellectually weak, and we find that Bob, the science teacher is not intellectually weak but intellectually sharp, then we may validly conclude that Bob was not educated in a college of education.

Pattern 4: affirming the consequent
If A then B, B is affirmed, therefore A is affirmed.

If there is convincing evidence to show that a sound relationship exists between persons educated in a college of education and those persons being intellectually weak, and we find that Bob, the science teacher is intellectually weak, then we may not validly conclude that he was educated in a college of education. Other conditions and/or circumstances may be the precipitating factor and not the college of education.

It should be noted that two of the patterns yield valid forms (Pattern 1 and Pattern 3) while the other patterns yield invalid hypothetical forms (Patterns 2 and 4).

What is the form and what valid conclusions can you draw from the following argument, if any ?

Recently, three textbooks were dropped from the sixth-grade curriculum because a group of parents complained that the books presented evolution as a fact rather than as a theory. Another group complained that several texts, in current use, promoted racial and sexual stereotypes, but these books were not dropped. Clearly, parent groups have no right to influence text choices. Parents do not know enough about the issues and have no training in evaluating books. The parents have no clear or consistent criteria for their judgments. Moreover, their positions may be used by those in power within the educational system as an endorsement for their biases (Moore, McCann & McCann, 1985, 23).

Informal Fallacies

While the inference made in arguments (the argument's form) yield the argument's validity, the evidence offered for arguments (the argument's content) afford analysis of the argument's truth and relevance of premises. False or irrelevant premises (reasons) provide serious and damaging criticism of an argument even though the argument's structure (form) may be valid according the rules of logic. If an argument employs such errors, (informal fallacies), that is, the evidence offered to support the conclusion or claim is unsound, then a reasonable person ought not to be convinced by such an argument.

An *informal fallacy* is "a mistake that either distorts or shrouds the meaning of a statement. Informal fallacies have nothing to do with the logical form of a deductive argument" (Thompson, 1995, 103). Here is a list of some common errors in reasoning involving the truth and relevance of the content of an argument:

1. *An appeal to authority* - Persons sometimes give a reason or reasons for some conclusion based on an appeal to an authority, the prestige or respect commanded by a person or organization. For example, the conclusion in an argument is drawn that "the findings of science do nothing to undermine religious belief." The evidence offered for such a conclusion is "no less a physicist than Einstein himself testified that his discoveries only strengthened his religious convictions." Here the acceptance of a claim is being made on an appeal to the authority of a recognized expert instead of to the logically reasoned merits for supporting a particular point of view in an argument. When this is done the *fallacy of an appeal to authority* is committed.

2. *Argumentum ad hominem (mud slinging)* - Some persons will attempt to win an argument over what course of action to take in regard to a particular educational issue by trying to demean or slander the character or competence (or both) of those who oppose them. For example, a parent who is a proponent of the banning of certain textbooks from the public schools might argue that teacher Erskine Dottin, an opponent of the textbooks ban, cannot offer intellectual ideas on the matter because he is an educationist who speaks educationese. This would be a form of *argumentum ad hominem* or an argument directed against the person taking a position rather than an argument based on efforts to refute or disprove the specific reasons given for an opponent's point of view on an issue. In this error in reasoning, it is assumed by the person committing the error that anything that discredits a person discredits his/her views as well.

3. *Appeal to pity* - The evidence offered to support a conclusion is sometimes just simply an appeal to one's sympathies, feelings, and piety instead of to the more cogent argument. This kind of fallacy is known as an *appeal to pity*. For example, the error would be committed if a politician tried to use this argument: "ladies and gentlemen, we must return Senator Blue to her post in Washington, D.C. in the next election. In addition to the fact that she sacrificed a lucrative career in law to enter public service, she has recently suffered the tragedy of losing a daughter in an automobile accident."

4. *Non-sequitur (it does not follow)* - Sometimes people give reasons for their position on a particular matter, but these reasons, in fact, are not reasons for their position.

Instead, they are reasons for another position. In other words, these reasons or premises are totally irrelevant to the conclusion drawn. This error in reasoning is known as *non-sequitur* or in some cases *irrelevant reason*. An example of this kind of reasoning is seen in the following: (a) Student - "I tried hard in the examination; therefore, I should get an A in the class" (b) Student - "Professor Blank was born in Barbados, I am sure we shall find his views on the history of Barbados most interesting."

5. *Complex Question* - Sometimes persons ask questions in such a manner that certain prior questions are implied to be true or false. In other words, the question is framed so that a direct answer involves acceptance of a prior unanswered question. For example, if a principal were to ask a teacher being interviewed for a position "are you still advocating the use of corporal punishment in the classroom?" then the error here would be in the form of a leading and *complex question*. The question implies a prior unanswered question on the part of the principal.

6. *Begging the question* - Sometimes persons simply state the conclusion of an argument in changed form in the reasons (premises) offered. This error in reasoning is really reasoning in a circle, and is known as *begging the question*. An example of this fallacy may be gleaned from the following arguments: (a) Student - "there is no sense in blaming me for getting the lowest grade in Professor Dottin's exam--somebody had to get the lowest grade" (b) "This argument is fallacious. You can tell it is fallacious because it is not valid. It is not valid because it contains a fallacy."

7. *Appeals to catch the crowd* - Persons sometimes offer a cliché or slogan to catch the crowd as the basis of support for a particular conclusion. For example, the following argument commits this fallacy: "A million people can't all be wrong--this book has had a million readers." The error here is known as an argument *to catch the crowd*.

8. *Fallacy of composition (converse accident)* - The fallacy of composition is made when we assume that what is true of a part is also true of a whole. For example, to assume that because State University has eleven individually gifted football players that the university will automatically have a great football team may be an error.

On the other hand, the *fallacy of converse accident* is made when the assumption is made that what is true under some circumstances is true in general; exceptions are regarded as typical instances. For example, "Sunset High school has the smallest gym in the district; therefore, Sunset High must be a very small high school."

9. The *Fallacy of division (accident)* - The fallacy of division is the converse of the fallacy of composition. The fallacy of division is to reason that what is true of the whole is also true of the parts. If we reason that because the school band has a great sound then every member of the band is an accomplished musician then we commit the *fallacy of division*. On the other hand, some persons offer unqualified generalizations as the basis of support for an argument. In other words, facts relevant to the argument are not represented correctly in the premises. For example, if someone argued "I need no evidence to convince me that your lizard has been worrying my fly, for it is well known that lizards worry flies." This error in reasoning is known as the *fallacy of accident*.

Now let us return to the argument about Bob, the science teacher: Teachers who have been educated in colleges of education are intellectually weak. Bob, the science teacher at Millville High is intellectually sharp; as a result, I am sure he was not educated in a college of education. Do you detect any informal fallacies in reasoning? Do you detect the error of *begging the question*?

Bibliography

Aspy, D.N., Aspy, C.B., & Quimby, P.M. (1993). What doctors can teach teachers about problem-based learning. *Educational Leadership*, 50 (7), 22-24.

Birman, B.F., Desimone, L., Porter, A.C., & Garet, M. S. (May 2000). Designing professional development that works. *Educational Leadership*, 57 (8), 28 – 33.

Broudy, H.S. (Spring 1990). Case studies - why and how. *Teachers College Record*, 91 (3), 449-459.

Burton, W.H., Kimball, R.B. & Wing, R.L. (1960). *Education for effective thinking*. New York: Appleton-Century-Crofts.

Carnegie Commission (1986). A nation prepared: Teachers for the 21st century. New York: Carnegie Forum on Education and the Economy.

Carr, J. A. (1998). Information literacy and teacher education. ERIC, Digest #97-4. Retrieved from the World Wide Web: http://www.ericsp.org/97-4.html.

Clabaugh, G.K. & Rozycki, E.G. (1997). *Analyzing controversy: an introductory guide*. Sluice Dock, Guilford, CT.: Dushkin/McGraw-Hill.

Cochran-Smith, M. & Lytle, S.L. (1999). "Relationships of knowledge and practice: Teacher learning communities" in Asghar Iran-Nejad & P. David Pearson (Editors*). Review of research in education (*24), 249-305. Washington, D.C.: AERA.

Code of student conduct, Elementary. (Revised August 27, 1997). Miami-Dade County Public Schools, Alternative Education and Dropout Prevention, Board Rule 6Gx13-5D-1.08.

Connelly, F.M. & Elbaz, F. (1980). Conceptual bases for curriculum thought: A teacher's perspective. In A.W. Foshay (Ed.), *Considered action for curriculum improvement*. Alexandria, VA: Association for Supervision and Curriculum Development.

Contract between the Miami-Dade County Public Schools and the United Teachers of Dade, FEA/United, AFT, Local 1974, AFL-CIO. Effective July 1, 1999 through June 30, 2002.

Dewey, J. (1910). *How we think*. Boston: D.C. Heath & Co.

Doebler, L.K., Roberson, T. & Ponder, C.W. (1998). Preservice teacher case study responses: a preliminary attempt to describe program impact. *Education*, Winter, 119 (2).

---------- (March, 28, 1990). Teacher educators turn to case study method. *Education Week*, IX (27), 1, 19.

Dottin, E.S. (1984). The humanistic climate scale- 6 key elements for facilitating human development in democratic social environments. Pensacola, Fl.

Eggen, P.D. & Kauchak, D.P. (1988). *Strategies for teachers: teaching content and thinking skills.* 2nd ed. Englewood Cliffs, NJ: Prentice Hall.

Florio-Ruane, S., & Clark, C. (1990). Using case studies to enrich field experiences. *Teacher Education Quarterly,* 17 (1), 29-43.

Gardner, H. (1983). *Frames of mind: the theory of multiple intelligences.* New York: Basic Books.

Geiger, J.& Shugarman, S. (Fall 1988). Portfolios and case studies to evaluate teacher education students and programs. *Action in Teacher Education,* 10 (3), 31-34.

Goleman, D. (1995). *Emotional intelligence: why it can matter more than IQ.* New York: Bantam.

Goodlad, J. I. (November 1990). Better teachers for our nation's schools. *Phi Delta Kappan,* 72 (3), 185-194.

Greenwood, G., & Parkay, F. (1989). *Case studies for teacher decision-making.* New York: Random House.

Jackson, D. L. & Ormrod, J.E. (1998). *Case studies: applying educational psychology.* Columbus, Ohio: Merrill.

Kennedy, M. (1988). Establishing professional schools for teachers. In M. Levine (Ed.), *Professional practice schools: building a model.* Washington, D.C.: American Federation of Teachers.

Kohlberg, L. (1967). Moral and religious education and the public schools: a developmental view. In T. Sizer (Ed.), *Religion and public education.* Boston: Houghton Mifflin.

Kowalski, T.J., Weaver, R.A. & Henson, K.T. (1990). *Case studies on teaching.* New York: Longman.

Levine, D.U & Levine, R.F. (1996*). Society and education* 9th edition. Boston: Allyn & Bacon.

Maeroff, G. I. (1988). *The empowerment of teachers: overcoming the crisis of confidence.* New York: Teachers College Press.

McAninch, A. R. (1993). *Teacher thinking and the case method: theory and future directions.* New York: Teachers College Press.

Merseth, K.K. (June 1990). The case for cases in teacher education. Unpublished paper.

Miller, J. P. (January 1999). Making connections through holistic learning. *Educational Leadership,* 46-48.

Moles, O. C. (Ed.). (1996). *Reaching all families: creating family-friendly schools.* Office of Educational Research and Improvement, U.S. Department of Education.

Moore, W.E., McCann, H., & McCann, J. (1985). *Creative and critical thinking.* 2nd edition. Boston: Houghton Mifflin.

National Board for Professional Teaching Standards (October, 1997). *Leading the way: 10 years of progress 1987-1997,* Washington, D.C.

National Institute on Educational Governance, Finance, Policy Making, and Management. (April, 1998). High performance learning communities: a new vision for American schools, in *The Policy Forum,* 1(2), 1-4.

Parent and family education program (2000-2001). Kindergarten Parent/Child Transitional Activities Calendar. Miami-Dade County Public Schools, Miami, Florida.

Pettig, K. L. (September, 2000). On the road to differentiated practice. *Educational Leadership,* 58 (1), 14 -19.

Professional Assessment And Comprehensive Evaluation System PACES Pilot 2000, Teaching and learning professional growth manual. (Draft 6/9/2000), for use in M-DCPS Pilot Schools, 2000-2001.

Pupil Progression Plan (1999). Miami-Dade County Public Schools, Elementary, Secondary, and Workforce Development Education. Board Rule 6Gx 13-5B-1.04.

Ruder, S. (September, 2000). We teach all. *Educational Leadership,* 58, (1), 49 – 51.

Ruggiero, V.R. (Summer 2000). Bad attitude: confronting the views that hinder students' learning. *American Educator,* American Federation of Teachers, 10 – 15.

Savery, J. (1994, May). What is problem-based learning? Paper presented at the meeting of the Professors of Instructional Design and Technology, Indiana State University, Bloomington, IN.

Shulman, L., & Colbert, J. (1988). The intern teacher casebook. Eugene, Oregon: ERIC Clearinghouse on Educational Management, Educational Research and Development; Washington, D.C: ERIC Clearinghouse on Teacher Education.

Shulman, L. (1989). A case for cases. (Speech). Monterey, CA.: Project 30.

Silverman, R., Welty, W. M., & Lyon, S. (1992). *Case studies for teacher problem solving.* New York: McGraw-Hill.

Strong families, strong schools: building community partnerships for learning. (1994). A research base for family involvement in learning from the U.S. Department of Education.

Suhor, C. (January 1999).   Spirituality—letting it grow in the classroom. *Educational Leadership,* 12-16.

Thompson, L.J. (1995). *Habits of the mind: critical thinking in the classroom.* Lanham: University Press of America.

Wehrmann, K. S. (September, 2000). Baby steps: a beginner's guide. *Educational Leadership,* 58, (1), 20 – 23.

AUTHORS' BIOGRAPHICAL SKETCHES

Erskine Sylvester Dottin is a 1976 Miami University of Ohio, Ph.D. graduate. He is currently a member of the Department of Educational Foundations and Professional Studies at Florida International University, Miami, Florida. His teaching responsibilities include undergraduate and graduate courses in social foundations of education.

He has been a member of the American Educational Studies Association for some 22 years, assuming leadership roles for that association with the Committee on Academic Standards and Accreditation, and the association's Executive Council. He was the inaugural President of the Florida Foundations of Education and Policy Studies Society, and has served as an officer of the Southeast Philosophy of Education Society. He is currently President of the Council of Learned Societies in Education, and serves as a member of the National Council for Accreditation of Teacher Education (NCATE) Board of Examiners and the NCATE Unit Accreditation Board. He was an active member of the Unit Accreditation Board's NCATE 2000 Standards Committee, the committee responsible for writing the NCATE 2000 Standards.

His research interest is in the area of humanistic/holistic education. His articles have appeared in the *Florida Journal of Teacher Education, Teacher Education Quarterly, College Student Journal, Educational Foundations Journal, Journal of Humanistic Education* and *Holistic Education* (now *Encounter: Education for Meaning and Social Justice*).

He has edited, *The Forum,* and co-authored *Thinking About Education: Philosophical Issues and Perspectives,* and *Teaching as Enhancing Human Effectiveness.* His book reviews have appeared in *Choice, Educational Studies Journal, Journal for Students Placed at Risk,* and the *Journal of Negro Education.*

Mickey Weiner graduated from the University of Wisconsin-Madison in 1982 with a Bachelor of Science in Elementary Education. She received a Master's in Reading in 1987 and a Doctorate in Education in the area of Curriculum and Instruction in 1997 from Florida International University.

She began teaching elementary school in 1983, and is currently teaching fifth grade at North Hialeah Elementary School in Miami, Florida. Her teaching experience has included grades K-9. She has been an adjunct professor at Florida International University and taught at the graduate level in the College of Education (1997-1999).

She has had leadership experience at the district level of Miami-Dade County Public Schools where she is an Eisenhower resource teacher in the area of mathematics and a teacher program assistant for PACES (Professional and Comprehensive Evaluation System).

She became a national board certified teacher in 1999 and enjoys mentoring others who are involved in the process. She is a member of the United Teachers of Dade (UTD), and is currently enrolled in its Future Leaders Program. Other member affiliations include Dade Reading Council, International Reading Association, National Council of Teachers of Mathematics, and National Council for the Social Studies.

LIST OF CONTRIBUTORS

Carol Bregman was born in Brooklyn, New York but has lived most of her life in South Florida. She currently teaches a self contained gifted class of fifth and sixth graders at South Pointe Elementary on Miami Beach. She attended Florida State University where she received her degree in Social Science. Later, Carol became certified in elementary education and endorsed in gifted education through courses taken at Florida International University.

Rebecca Francis was born in Indiana but has lived and taught for the last 26 years in South Florida. She currently teaches third grade at South Pointe Elementary on Miami Beach. She received her bachelor's degree in elementary education from Ball State University and her master's degrees in reading and urban education from Florida International University.

Cynthia Lasky was born in Waterbury, Connecticut. She received her bachelor's degree in elementary education from the University of Southern Connecticut. Cynthia has lived in Florida since 1970. She attended Barry University where she received her master's degree in reading, and Nova University where she received her doctorate degree in early middle childhood education. She is retiring from the Miami-Dade County Public School System after 30 years as a classroom teacher and lead teacher. She is now employed as an assistant professor of education at Barry University.

Mariolga Lebredo was born in Havana, Cuba but grew up in Milwaukee, Wisconsin. In 1986 she moved to Florida where she has been teaching art for the past 14 years in the Miami-Dade County Public School System, the last nine at South Pointe Elementary on Miami Beach. Mariolga graduated from the University of Wisconsin with a bachelor's degrees in Art Education and Spanish. She received her master's degree in College Student Personnel Administration from Western Illinois University. She has completed all coursework leading to the specialist degree in exceptionalities with licensing in gifted education at Nova Southeastern University. She has worked as an Area Coordinator for the Department of Residential Life at Central Missouri State University (1983-85), and as a Bilingual Educational Counselor for the Department of Higher Education in Wisconsin (1985-86).

Bertha Moro was born in Havana, Cuba, but has been a South Florida resident for the past 41 years. She has taught for the Miami-Dade County Public School System at the elementary level for 14 years. She recently accepted a principal position at St. Patrick Parish School in Miami Beach and is currently finishing her master's in administration.

Judy Newman was raised in Miami, Florida, where she and her husband also reared their three children. She received a Bachelor of Science in Elementary Education from Barry University, and a Master's of Science in Early Childhood Education from the University of Miami. She has taught in the Miami-Dade County Public Schools for over 18 years. She is currently a Pre-K/Early Intervention teacher on Miami Beach, as well as an adjunct professor at Barry University.

Doris Olesky was born in New York City. She graduated with a B.A. in secondary education from Georgian Court College, Lakewood, New Jersey where she majored in English. She received certification in elementary education from Barry University, Miami, Florida. She earned a master's degree in Reading at Florida International University. Ms. Olesky has 25 years teaching experience ranging from kindergarten through high school. However, most of her time was spent in the elementary field. Her interests include antiques, travel, horticulture, healthful living, and children especially.